"Like many of us today, Byllye's life is one of commitment and too much to do. Stop, as I did when she sent me her lovely book, and meditate with her upon the words and feelings that touch and mend our hearts and souls."

—Marian Wright Edelman, President, The Children's Defense Fund

"*An Altar of Words* is like a wise friend to talk to everyday, guidance in both the external and internal worlds, and support in being your true self. Byllye Avery, a wise and loving woman herself, has gathered words to guide us all toward love, health, and wisdom."

—Gloria Steinem

"Speaking of words, this lovely volume is suffused with the wisdom, struggle, empathy, humor, strength, and generosity Byllye Avery embodies in this world. Like Byllye, the book is a precious gift to us all—to anyone able and willing to open her or his heart to a message of peace and of hope."

—Diana Chapman Walsh, Ph.D., President, Wellesley College

Wisdom, Comfort, and Inspiration

* * *

BROADWAY BOOKS

NEW YORK

An Altar of Words

BYLLYE AVERY

activism * agency * beauty * boogie dow * comfort * courage * dream * family * happines * heaven * joy * moon set * persever * moments * purple * sexuality * sister spirit * sisternomics * solitude * spirit * strength * trees * voice * water * wellness * will * wisdom

africa * balance * blessings * choice * nections * divine * free spirit * guidance * heart * integrity * mommy * passion * precious * pride * sacred * shalom * stillness

BROADWAY

GRATEFUL ACKNOWLEDGMENT IS MADE FOR PERMISSION TO REPRINT THE FOLLOWING:

Excerpt from "Poem For a Lady Whose Voice I Like" by Nikki Giovanni. Reprinted by permission of William Morrow and Company from *The Women and the Men* by Nikki Giovanni. Copyright 1975 by Nikki Giovanni.

Many other quotes in *An Altar of Words* are from the following:

The Black Woman's Gumbo Ya-Ya. Edited by Terri L. Jewell. The Crossing Press, 1993.
Famous Black Quotations. Edited by Janet Cheatham Bell. Warner Books, 1995.
Quotations By Women. Compiled and edited by Rosalie Maggio. Beacon Press, 1996.
Treasury of Women's Quotations. Edited by Carolyn Warner. Prentice Hall, 1992.
Victory of the Spirit. Edited by Janet Cheatham Bell. Warner Books, 1996.

Library of Congress Cataloging-in-Publication Data
Avery, Byllye, 1937–
An altar of words : wisdom, comfort, and inspiration / [Byllye Avery].
p. cm.
Originally published: New York: Broadway Books, 1998.
ISBN 0-7679-0080-4 (pbk.)
I. Afro-American women—Religious life. I. Title.
[BL625.2.A94   1999]
158'.082—dc21   98-39533
                                                           CIP

First trade paperback edition published 1999.

Designed by T. Karydes

99   00   01   02   03   10   9   8   7   6   5   4   3   2

This book is for my mother, L. Alyce M. Ingram.
Her love and devotion have sustained me. I love you.

I betook myself to prayer and in every lonely place I found an altar.

Elizabeth, bondswoman and minister,

born in Maryland, 1766

CONTENTS

Acknowledgments

Writing this book has been a blessing. The process has enabled me to gather and reflect on my experiences to understand their lessons more fully. I am grateful for the blessings of the universe and everyday opportunities to grow.

As I began to write this book, I asked groups of women to suggest words that I might include as altar contributions. They responded generously, giving me words that added richness to the list I chose to write about. While I was not able to use all of their contributions, I am grateful for their creative offerings and their supportive energy.

I recognize the word contributions of the following women:

The Healing Our Essence Spirituality Conference in Santa Barbara: Janet, Gini, Susan, Lynda, Corrine, Ann-Marie, Christina, Mary Anne, Elizabeth, Judy, Christine, Susan, LaDonna, Shan, Barbara, Stefanie, and Sharon.

The Infant Mortality Conference in Tampa: Betty, Kim, Penny, Skippy, Nancy, Bettye, Lydia, Sydney, Kimberly, Joyce, and Barrie.

The Domestic Violence Conference in Hershey: Marcia, Carron, Doreen, Bike, Cynthia, Stacy, and Affefa.

Mountainview Lake, New Hampshire: Wendy, Judy, Polly, Jewel, Cheryl, and Gwen.

*National Black Women's Health Project: Nzinga, Ngina,
Shriki, Fran, Holly, Sibongile, Akua, Barbara, Ama, and Julia.
Friends: Lynn, Jeannie, Diane, and Alexa.*

Blessings to all of the women of the National Black Women's Health Project who said, "Please write it, Byllye, we need it." So, here it is!

Thanks to Janet Goldstein for her sensitive editing and to Lynn Rosen for being a remarkable agent and a supportive friend. I continue to be grateful to Abby Moore for her loving support and mindful attention. A special thanks to A. J. Verdelle for a big TA, and Lucinda for encouragement.

Love and appreciation to my family Wesley, Sonja, Angela, and to Ngina for her love, support, and willingness to struggle with me on the difficult words.

Introduction

Altars have always been special places to me. In Bethel African Methodist Episcopal Church in De Land, Florida, where I grew up, there was a small, simple altar in front of the pulpit. On the first Sunday of each month, the altar, draped in white, held bright silver communion trays of bread and wine. We approached and knelt at the altar to receive the holy sacrament from the minister. This ritual act emphasized the holiness of this place. We respected it.

Another altar that comes to mind is at Talladega College in Alabama, where I went to school. On the floor of the library is a mosaic of the insurgent Amistad slave ship. The revolt led to a lengthy trial that freed the Africans. We honored its legacy by not walking upon the ship's mosaic likeness. By this act of respect, we made it an altar.

An altar is a sacred place for reflection, self-examination, and renewal. Altars provide a refuge, offering safety and solace while we explore the spirit within us.

Many of us have meaningful objects in our homes that serve as spiritual offerings. When we group them in a special place we create an altar. I have my altar in my bedroom, covered with many articles, each with a story or memory. A strip of kente reminds me of a dear departed friend; seashells remind me of a memorable beach sunset. A purple glass pyramid graces my altar, along with a special doll given to me as an award. Altars can be created any place in the home. We anoint a space and declare it sacred. In creating an altar, we are only limited by our minds.

An altar of words provides an opportunity to create a verbal sacred space. Our close examination and reflection transforms words into objects with significance and meaning that can be placed on the altar. Words are powerful. They express our feelings, evoke emotions, and give voice to our experiences. Each word summons a different experience or possibility.

Love forms the foundation of the altar. The presence of love allows us to be present and experience all emotions.

When we build an altar of words, we create a sanctuary in the mind that prepares us for meditation and reflection. As you examine each word in the safety of your thoughts, think about how the word applies to your life and your reality. These thoughts give you permission to make changes or accept present realities. A verbal altar provides you with guidance directed by your inner spirit and healing energy.

Each of us progresses along the road of life differently. Build your altar following the cadence of your heart and soul. Some words may take a day to reflect upon, while others will take longer. You can determine how much time is needed to spend with your inner self. This book is my altar. It is the pulse of my heart and soul. My thoughts, experiences, and life lessons are my gifts to you and the universe.

Activism

Just when does one decide to devote her life or some part of her life to activism? I can't recall ever hearing a child say, "I want to be an activist when I grow up." What transforms regular, hard-working citizens into dedicated, passionate activists? Perhaps it is anger fuming in the blood that makes us resist the injustices hurled at members of society. Perhaps it is the high standards of excellence that we hold for our society, to be better than the best, with integrity and respect for everyone. Whatever the cause, we never know when the moment will come that an issue emerges as a burning passion and we commit ourselves to making sure the world knows about "our" issue.

Activists help make the world a better place. Many important changes have been made because something clicked and made people see the picture more clearly, focusing on the vision of what could be, and how changes can lead to a better society. We must celebrate our activists. They are trailblazers who are not afraid to speak out, stand up, and challenge the status quo. They do their work today, and create a place for volunteers later. Activism leads and inspires change. The activist's passion provides a driving force for the rest of us.

I became an activist in the early '70s. The women's health movement was in full swing, making us all think about health in terms of personal involvement and control. My husband had a massive heart attack and died in 1970, and I realized that as an educated Black person I knew very little about health and taking care of myself.

I began to educate myself, and I dedicated more and more time to working on women's health issues. Before I knew it, health had become my issue and my full-time job.

We all have some parts of activism within us. Very few people don't have strong feelings about something. Some of us are quiet activists, keeping our feelings to ourselves and using our quiet strength and resources to advance our issues. We all need to seek ways to be activists and support activism.

As you add **activism** to your altar, think about and feel the passion of an issue that is important to you.

My actions are important and are
inherently powerful.

"Dissension is healthy, even when it gets loud."
Jennifer Lawson

Africa

For many African Americans, traveling to Africa is an emotional and sacred experience. When I made my first trip to Africa in 1985 to attend the UN Conference on Women, I felt excited and privileged. The warmth, caring, and spirit of the African people was incredible and overpowering. We were welcomed home and felt in touch with previous generations as we shared in our hosts' culture and food, and wrapped ourselves in the beautiful colors of African fabric.

When we arrived in Nairobi, our National Black Women's Health Project delegation of twenty-five women joined more than three thousand African American women at this historic conference. Most of us had not attended an event with women from all over the African continent, let alone women from all over the world. The conference had its usual fare of informative workshops, but the sharing of our life stories was where the real learning took place. We found commonalities in our different lives. We taught each other songs and dances, and the African women identified our ancestral tribes by our facial features and gave us names. We were touched by one another's spirits and souls.

The most impressive thing about Africa to me, other than the beauty of the continent, is the spirit of the people. Despite the poverty, the treatment of women, and the lack of opportunities, there is a quality of self-respect, honor, and creativity that holds many answers for us. Our connections with women at the conference brought us face-to-face with our struggles and triumphs. We emerged feeling healthier and connected.

As you place **Africa** on the altar, feel connected across time and space.

I know that Africa provides me with power and connections. I rejoice in recognizing my heritage.

"It's impossible to love ourselves without having an attraction to Africa."
Randall Robinson, President, TransAfrica

Agency

Regarding the relationship between people and the universe, it is clear that we are all conduits for the sharing of knowledge, power, and energy. Each of us has something to contribute that is unique and enlightening. Each of us has agency. Agency is the power within us to change ourselves and the world around us. Connecting with our sense of agency takes us on a lifelong journey of empowerment—for ourselves and others. Agency is one of our most precious gifts . . . and one of our most awesome responsibilities.

We embrace agency each time we take a child's hand to lead, teach a person to read, reach out to help, or listen in an active, supportive way. Active listening is a gift that enables us to support each other in a special way. It requires that we be present and listening, while the energy of attention works its healing powers.

We extend the gift of agency by becoming a conduit for a course of action. Eye contact and supportive nods—without interruptions—silently let the person know you hear her loud and clear. The affirmation of presence helps each of us hear our inner answers to our questions, see the path to solutions, and visualize ourselves in a better place. Talking, listening, seeing, and feeling create the conduit for change and growth—the primary mission of agency.

As you place **agency** on the altar, think of ways you have been an agent and a receiver. Keep the energy of that feeling with you throughout the day.

I am an agent of the universe and I delight
in sharing.

"We must light the paths and lighten the load for each other."
Judith Levy (dear friend who died of breast cancer in 1987)

Anger

Anger makes us feel warm and passionate. It can also make us feel scared and out of control when we forget that it is a normal feeling that expresses displeasure.

For many years, I was very afraid of anger, my own as well as that of others. I thought the expression of anger meant that I was being rejected or not liked. It has taken years for me to learn that a person can be angry with me and still love me. In order to attend to someone's anger, each person needs to know that trust and caring will survive angry expressions.

There are many great things that emerge from anger and rage. The civil rights and women's movements are good examples. The civil rights movement helped us understand that anger could be expressed in many ways, facing violence with nonviolence. We were also forced to deal with our inner rage, and to deal with our fears, misconceptions, and contradictions. We learned how deeply racial prejudices and attitudes are embedded into the fabric of America's psyche. The anger of the women's movement forced us to look at all parts of our lives—our work, our homes, our health care, and our relationships.

Unexpressed anger is dangerous. It seeps out in passive-aggressive ways that can be destructive and nonproductive. Repressed anger can lead to physical and emotional illness. It is crucial that we learn to express this powerful emotion, recover, and get on with life.

We express anger because we hurt and we care deeply. These expressions keep us sane and whole.

As you place **anger** on the altar, feel the warmth and relief that this emotion offers.

I recognize anger as an emotion that needs to be expressed and listened to.

"Anger is loaded with information and energy."
Audre Lorde, "The Uses of Anger," *Sister Outsider* (1984)

Balance

Each New Year's eve, among all the resolutions, we vow to take more time to enjoy life, to put ourselves in the equation, and to spend more time with the people we love. But, before we know it, we are wishing once again that each day had just one more hour. We need balance. We need to create a cycle that includes work, rest, and play.

Start by reconsidering play. Yes, the play we loved to do as children, when we lost ourselves in imaginary worlds and escaped to a timeless utopia. Think about the relationship between play, exercise, and relaxation that gives us energy to keep going strong and feeling good. A day on the beach reminds us of the relaxing combination of sun, sand, and water. And wouldn't it be great if we took time to play softball, basketball, volleyball, or golf, to go swimming or Rollerblading, or to learn a new game that could give us much pleasure as we exercise with others? This is a great outlet for a new discovery of oneself and others.

Rest means complete relaxation, freeing the mind and body to do nothing so it can repair and become recharged. Sit outside on a warm breezy day; quietly meditate in a room by yourself; enjoy a relaxing bath. Spend time doing nothing. Go ahead—it is okay. We must unlearn the ethic that says we are being lazy when we take time to rest. Plan to go to bed on time—just because stores are open all night you don't have to do those errands, or because television stations broadcast all night you don't have to watch. Rest is important and necessary.

Work is necessary because it makes survival possible. Yet many of us are bored or hate our jobs. We would rather be almost anywhere else. If this is your situation then try and find a job that you love doing, even if you make a little less money. This satisfaction will enable you to be more productive and could enhance your opportunities for advancement. It is also good to be able to leave work at work when you come home, so if you are a person who worries a lot or carries a great deal of stress you should try and work a job that is completed at the end of each day. Or you can set your daily goals of what is reasonable to be accomplished and enjoy a sense of completion at day's end.

You can determine what is a balanced life and proceed to

achieve it. Balance can bring peace, happiness, and contentment. It might not be achieved overnight, but it will never happen unless you start today.

As you place **balance** on the altar, think about one thing you can do to make your life more balanced.

Balance is necessary for my well-being. I will work to make it an essential part of my life.

"When you're following your energy and doing what you want all the time, the distinction between work and play dissolves."

Shakti Gawain, *Living in the Light* (1986)

Beauty

Seeing and being in the midst of beauty makes me feel good. I love having beautiful things around me: flowers, art, and other lovely things to look at. Flowers can instantly transform space and feelings. I made a decision several years ago to always have fresh flowers in my life and I buy them weekly.

Often our environment influences our mood, so we need to make our days as pleasant as possible. Think about how good it feels to go to the ocean where the beautiful surroundings help us feel good about ourselves and clean out the cobwebs of our minds.

When I was a child, my mother read to me and provided me with lots of illustrated books, which I loved. I did the same for my children, to teach them to appreciate beauty in art. When we surround ourselves with art, the beauty that we behold makes us think pleasant thoughts about ourselves. So if you see a piece of art that makes you feel good, that is a good enough reason to buy it. It will make you feel good each time you see it. Place beautiful things in strategic places and incorporate their spirit into your being.

We also must think about the beauty inside ourselves, because this is the most important source of everlasting beauty. The saying is true: "Beauty is as beauty does." We do not know you are beautiful unless we are able to see it through your actions. We all have the potential and the power to use and display our inner beauty.

As you place **beauty** on the altar, feel your inner beauty and reflect on a beautiful object.

I have inner beauty and I am deserving of the pleasurable satisfaction it gives me.

"We 'ourselves' are high art."
Ntozake Shange

Belonging

When my first cousin's daughter said to me, "I know we are kin, but I don't know how we are related," I knew we had some family work to do. At the next family gathering, I took along a laptop computer with family tree software and recorded our family's history. At the end of two days we had recorded seven generations of relatives, listened to hundreds of funny stories, talked about family illnesses and deaths, and discovered the richness of our connections. We strengthened our sense and feelings of belonging.

We stand on the shoulders of our ancestors as we support future generations. Knowing where we come from helps us determine where we are going. We all belong somewhere and to someone; interconnections help establish our roots. We did not come along alone: we are joined to each other by the lines of life.

We belong to a global community, are connected to a human family tree, and are all one another's kin. Acceptance of ourselves and one another is a uniting force that helps us understand our connectedness in diversity, our similarities and our differences. When we honor our global connections we ground ourselves in humanity.

Take time to appreciate yourself and your connections. Make it a priority to appreciate life, and expect and demand tolerance of yourself and others.

Think of people who provide you with a strong sense of connection when you place **belonging** on the altar.

I am a part of a global family and I feel connections to my personal being.

"Call it a clan, call it a network, call it a tribe, call it a family. Whatever you call it, whoever you are, you need one."
Jane Howard, *Families* (1978)

Blessings

In her book, *Don't Block the Blessings*, Patti LaBelle writes about the importance of recognizing one's blessings, claiming them, creating positive energy, and enjoying all that they bestow upon us. She reminds us to look at ourselves carefully, evaluate our gifts and talents, be grateful, and allow the blessings to flow.

Take time to count some of your blessings, the things we often take for granted: awakening in the morning, the gift of health, security, food on the table, loving family and friends. We come to expect that we have certain things present in our lives and that they will always be there. Few things are promised and everything can and will change. By appreciating the present we recognize our vulnerabilities and acknowledge the generosity of the universe.

As we start to think about our relationships, it is important to tell people how we feel about them. Take time to say "I love you." If there is something pressing that you haven't found the right time to say, find the time now. When we hold back, we close off the blessings we have to give. We also hold back the potential for any blessings we might receive. A few words can clear up a lot of confusion and provide healing.

When we open ourselves to the universe and know that every act and deed has a purpose, we are able to allow our blessings to flow. We are able to recognize ourselves as loving, caring, and whole persons. As we start to claim all of who we are and to become comfortable with ourselves, our blessings grow and we become prosperous in our spirit.

As you place **blessings** on the altar, recognize yours and be grateful.

I am blessed and I rejoice in my bountifulness.

"My fear of change caused me a lot of anguish and heartache until I learned to accept some simple facts of life: change is the only constant—the trick is to learn to see it as just another opportunity to grow, a chance to transform yourself from the person you are into the person you want to be. When you fear it, you fight it. And when you fight it, you block the blessing."

Patti LaBelle, *Don't Block the Blessings* (1996)

Boogie Down

When did you first learn to dance? Can you remember the moment you let go of being self-conscious and let it all hang out all over the floor? I learned how to dance in the kitchen with the broom. This ever-present partner taught me the ins and outs of making smooth, quick turns as I was being swept away by hot energizing sounds. Dancing is healing.

There's a great energy created when the music is good and everyone can groove and boogie down. There's something sweet about the mustiness, and the fragrance gives permission to cut it. Boogie down is physically and psychically healing. Boogie down is about letting go of worries and stress by entering a special space. It's about losing yourself temporarily so you can find renewed spirit. We can feel this freedom when we allow our minds to let go, think those wonderful thoughts we don't usually allow our-selves to think. Just the idea of dancing like this is a turn on.

As you place **boogie down** on the altar, think of the last time you let go while dancing and allow your thoughts to revitalize you.

I fully accept my renewed spirit and restored energy.

"There are short-cuts to happiness, and dancing is one of them."
Vicki Baum, *I Know What I'm Worth* (1964)

Breath

The world is so full of stress that sometimes the only way we can deal with it is to hold our breath and plunge in. It's like taking a dive into water hoping that everything will be all right when you finally come up for air. Yet there are too many crises going on daily for us not to breathe, or to pay attention to our breathing. By breathing deeply when we are stressed, we create healing energy for our body. This release of tension gives us a moment of relaxation and helps us regroup and prepare for the next challenge.

Deep breathing is an integral part of meditation. By focusing on our breathing, we shut out all other stimuli and use our awareness attention for self-healing. I have a friend who has almost gotten rid of her migraine headaches by meditating twenty minutes daily. Healing abdominal breaths can reduce the general body tension that leads to anxiety and depression. Breathing is a natural healing power.

When we take the time to exhale, we focus on ourselves and our needs. But a moment is not enough—most of us need a longer time. So build in some time just to listen to your breathing. When you are stuck in traffic, when you feel anger building—breathe. When the phone is getting on your nerves, breathe.

Breathe before you start to pay your bills. Remember that breathing cleanses the body and invigorates your spirit.

As you place **breath** on the altar, take a few minutes, listen to your breathing, and experience its healing energy.

I will pay attention to my breathing and its healing energy.

"When you hold the breath, you hold the soul."
B. K. S. Iyengar, *Light on Yoga* (1966)

Change

I grew up as a scared little girl in De Land, Florida. I was shy and fearful of almost everything and everybody. My high school graduation picture has me seated between two people, both with their shoulders covering mine. I didn't have the gumption to square my shoulders.

When I became a widow with two children in 1970, I realized that in order to survive and prosper, I'd have to be a different person in the world. I would have to stop being so afraid and adopt a take-charge attitude.

Change brings about such mixed feelings: excitement, fear, joy. Change provides us with experiences that we convert to personal power.

Sometimes, when I'm in the midst of what is surely a "lesson," I find myself saying, "I hope I get this lesson right this time because I don't want this one again." Change is a challenge that provides us with opportunity to grow.

One way to embrace change and get support is by joining a self-help group. These groups provide a safe place for us to share and listen to ourselves and others. The sharing of your story with active listeners fills us with new insights and provides a healing process that facilitates change. You cannot change the world, but you can change yourself, and when you change yourself you change the way the whole world relates to you.

As you place **change** on the altar, think of a significant way in which you have changed.

I am in charge of my life and responsible for my growth and change.

"You know that you can't really make much of a difference in things until you change yourself."
Alice Walker

Choice

Reproductive freedom and choice loom heavily in the psyche of American society. Political pressure is placed on a woman who exercises her right to choose whether or not to bear children, and very little interest or support is offered to her in the implementation of her decision.

Making a decision to bear a child means a lifetime commitment to providing emotional, financial, and spiritual support for the child. Families need to have support to rear healthy children. Parenting is our most important job, and the future depends on adequate parenting. Yet thousands of wanted Black babies die each year, simply because our society, with its advanced technological health care system, cannot provide the basic needs to families that will ensure that these wanted children can thrive and survive. Black infant mortality in the United States is more of a social problem than a medical problem. Social support could go a long way toward helping these families rear the children they have chosen to bear.

Support is also needed for women and their families who choose not to bear children. The decision to have an abortion can be a difficult one, and while it might be the best option, that doesn't make it less difficult. Some women will experience emotional pain after they have made this decision, and they should be encouraged to heal and not be made to feel guilty about exercising their reproductive choice.

For almost half of my life, I have worked to ensure a woman's right to have reproductive choices. In the early days, I did not understand that abortion was so prevalent in the African American community. I became involved because of the large numbers of African American women who were dying from self-induced and illegal abortions. I was shocked to learn that Black women seek this service in disproportionate numbers. I learned that women make decisions based on the reality of their life situations, and their decision will vary depending on what is happening in their lives.

As I became involved with establishing a birthing center, I gained a different kind of respect for reproductive choice. It was a wonderful opportunity to work with families who were excited about their upcoming births and to share the zest with which they embraced pregnancy, childbearing, and child-rearing. Many were transformed by this highly spiritual experience. They were ready to contribute to humanity.

Choice is a cornerstone of our society. We claim pride in our abilities to make decisions about our lives. When women make reproductive choices they learn the power and control choice gives them in all areas of their lives. Reproductive choice provides control, builds self-esteem and confidence, and should not be taken for granted.

As you place **choice** on the altar, think about the value of choice in your life.

I value my right to make choices and respect
the rights of others.

"It is the ability to choose which makes us human."
Madeleine L'Engle, *Reflections on Faith and Art* (1980)

Comfort

I grew up with a big overstuffed chair in my bedroom and I remember fondly how it would wrap its arms around me, offering me unconditional comfort. It was a place to go to read, cool out, cry when I was hurt, and from time to time, I would pile it high with unironed clothes. We need to surround ourselves with things that make us feel safe and secure.

Clothes also need to be comfortable, especially shoes. Life is most unbearable when our feet hurt or our clothes fit too tight. I was amazed that the same men who made high-heeled shoes for women made comfortable commonsense shoes for men. It is a blessing to be comfortable wearing sensible shoes and clothes.

We need to have a source of comfort. We need to be able to talk to a friend, cry on someone's shoulder, and receive her caring love. Just as a kiss can make a child's bruise feel better, an attentive ear and a hug can make pain tolerable. When we offer comfort, we say "I love you and I care."

As you place **comfort** on the altar, imagine yourself surrounded by love.

When I am distressed I will lay down my troubles
and be comforted.

"I love it—I love it, and who shall dare/
To chide me for loving that old arm-chair?"
Eliza Cook, "The Old Arm-Chair" (1848)

Commitment

In 1972 I visited Australia and spent a week in an Aboriginal community outside of Sydney. I walked the streets, visited a preschool, shopped at markets, sat on porches talking to people who were as curious about me as I was about them, and enjoyed the differences between their culture and mine. We talked about everything from raising kids to politics, and I found the perspective of these gentle people to be so spiritual, and their thinking about life so advanced and yet basic. We talked a long time about learning, and when and how it should take place. They questioned the idea of children sitting indoors to learn about the world outdoors. I found their conversations to be challenging and in direct contradiction to many things I have been taught to value.

There were a lot of children in this community, so I asked if illegitimacy was a problem. They asked what did that mean, and I said, children who are born without fathers. They replied, "Oh, can you do that in the States now?" The idea of a child not having a father was a foreign idea and it made me realize that no person is fatherless, unlawful, illegal, or unacceptable. People are not disposable. We all belong to the global village and we are all committed to taking care of one another.

As we entered into a woman's modest home, I was told that she always held a small dog on her lap, but on that day she held a baby. She told us it was her cousin's baby and she was keeping it while the cousin was away. When my new Aboriginal friend asked her how long the woman would be gone, she said she didn't know. I tried to ask casually if she thought she would be gone a day or month or what. The woman said, "I really don't know, but I made a commitment to keep the baby until she returns, and the baby will stay with me until she comes back." I realized that commitment to one another is a value that undergirds this culture and it is taken seriously.

It is so important that we know the full meaning of a commitment when we make one. We often perceive of a commitment as a short-term activity and become upset when the time exceeds our expectations. We must be able to think through a situation and be comfortable knowing that the task may be more difficult and take a longer time to complete than expected. These realizations will make keeping the commitment more manageable.

As you place **commitment** on the altar, recognize that it comes with responsibility.

I make a commitment to myself which connects with my personal responsibilities.

"Nothing strengthens the judgment and quickens the conscience like individual responsibility."
Elizabeth Cady Stanton, *Solitude of the Self* (1892)

Connections

It's interesting how weather conditions can create time for families to be together. Some of my fondest childhood memories contain lasting images of the wind and fury of hurricanes. I remember how excited we were just at the thought of a storm a'coming. We would scurry to the grocery store, to make sure we had enough food, and locate the candles, Sterno, flashlights, books, games, the radio and batteries. And then all of the family went inside and stayed inside together. I loved to stare out the window, with my nose pressed to the glass, listening to the symphony created by the sound of the rain and mystified by the power and force of the wind.

Our family grew closer during these times. There was an amazing calmness in the house while a storm raged outside. We all had enough time to play games, read, and listen to my parents' stories of past hurricanes. This was a time when we all had permission to do nothing, which created a serenity as peaceful as the eye of the storm.

Family retreats provide us with the opportunity to see and feel each other with different eyes and arms. Good time family gatherings help us build strength to cope with the difficult life challenges. Quiet times allow us to reflect and engage in meaningful dialogue that can provide information and insight.

By allowing ourselves to show our vulnerabilities, we provide an opportunity to build and increase trust. Children become secure in the knowledge that families can and will provide guidance, support, and love in good and bad times, and they learn that this is the meaning of family. The storms of life can provide us with an opportunity to grow and develop inner calm and peace.

As you place **connections** on the altar, think of special times that you felt family closeness, peace, and love.

I am a member of the family of the universe;
I rejoice in my inclusion.

"This feeling of being loved and supported by the universe in general and by certain recognizable spirits in particular is bliss."

Alice Walker

Courage

We hear about people who are praised publicly for courageous acts, yet many of us commit acts of courage every single day of our lives. We go through life being afraid, yet we still face each and every single day, doing the very best we can at every given moment. We have courage throughout our lives and it comes to the forefront without much planning or thought.

We can also commit courageous acts at any age of our lives. Children are capable of performing heroic deeds, carrying out impossible tasks in the face of danger, simply because it was the right thing to do. Many of us are of great courage and we don't even know it. Facing our fears daily is truly an act of courage and an affirmation of our power.

As you put **courage** on the altar, know that courage makes possibilities into realities. It takes real courage to say to others that you are going to take time for yourself. That you are going to put yourself in the equation. Know that you are really worth it. Courage is healing.

I will put barriers behind me so I can realize
my possibilities.

*"The bravest thing you can do when you are not brave
is to profess courage and act accordingly."*
Corra Harris

Death

My brother died the last day of 1996. I remember the day he was born. It was hot that August day in 1945 when Mrs. Henrietta Griffin, the midwife, came to tell me that I had a baby brother. I was almost five years old. I can still see my mother's face in a glow of childbirth with my tiny brother in her arms. He was so little and red and my mother was so proud.

It is hard losing a loved one, especially one whose life was abbreviated by chronic illness. The multiple sclerosis that attacked his body in his twenties was finally diagnosed, after much suffering, twenty years later. Although he had completed law school, his illness made it impossible for him to practice this profession the way he had longed to do since childhood.

Quitman was a husband and father to two children who loved him dearly. He was able to parent children, upon whom he became totally dependent in later years for all of his needs. And yet my brother suffered his illness in silence. When asked how he was feeling he always said, "I can't complain," although he had plenty to complain about. It is difficult to see a loved one who uses silent suffering as a coping mechanism, especially when others of us scream and make noise. From my perspective he had a lot to be angry about—the disease, not practicing law, and a daily decrease in his quality of life. Yet he never said any complaining words.

Death came in the morning as a blessing to my brother and left us full of unspoken sadness and unshared thoughts. I remembered our childhood days in Florida, especially the Donald Duck cap that he gave my mother as a Mother's Day gift with the hopes that she would give it back to him. She kept it. He also loved cats and he named one Rosa Mae. When my mother told him the cat was a boy and needed to be renamed, he said, "I named her Rosa Mae and she turned to a boy, but she is Rosa Mae right on." I live with the memories of his laugh, his humor, and his caring spirit.

As you place **death** on your altar, think about birth and spirit and connecting memories.

I know that birth and death are a part of my reality and I affirm the presence of the spirit.

"Death in its way comes just as much of a surprise as birth."
Edna O'Brien, "Mrs. Reinhardt" (1978)

Denial

When reality is too difficult, it is easy to seek the seeming comfort of denial. It is so hard to face facts sometimes. Denial makes it possible to survive. But even though denial often seems like the easy choice, it often makes things harder. Our society is in denial about the extent of the disease of addiction. We just can't believe it, though we feel the pain and destruction that it has cost families and communities. Our denial has caused the problem of drug addiction to paralyze our criminal justice system. Addiction spans all generations. Gambling, alcoholism, sex, workaholism, food, and smoking are some addictions that harm individuals and society. Addiction is a disease, similar to diabetes, one that can be treated but not cured. It is not a source of shame, but it needs treatment. It is our responsibility to provide help, because we are one another's keepers.

Denial masks many signs and symptoms. It keeps us from dealing with lumps in our breasts, or from believing that we can get lung cancer from smoking or that unprotected sexual activity can lead to unintentional pregnancy and diseases. Denial provides us with a false sense of security.

Acceptance and awareness are the first stages of gaining the courage to change. They represent our first face-to-face meeting with denial and rejecting its silent voice. As we face our personal realities, we gain a better understanding of the process of change. These experiences enable us to become positive forces in the lives of others. As we face and deal positively with the reality of the present we gain control of our future actions.

Think deeply about an issue you are denying, and seek courage while you place **denial** on the altar.

I acknowledge the truths within me.

"The true believer begins with herself."
Berber proverb

Divine

Divine—what a glorious and sacred word! Divinity is the special quality that makes us unique: our presence, our love, our creative energy, and the ways in which we transform our environment.

There are many ways we can feel divine. It is a supreme experience of peace and pleasure. Chocolate lovers say biting into a luscious piece of chocolate is divine. We can feel divine when we have on just the right dress, you know, the one that hits all of the right places and makes us look a certain way. It gives us a divine, unparalleled feeling.

Can you remember the last time everything you wanted to happen fell right in place? The moments feel like a blessing from the universe. The sacred lives within each of us; we all have the capacity to be divine.

Starhawk, in her book *Truth or Dare*, reminds us that each being is sacred—that each person has inherent value that cannot be ranked in a hierarchy or compared to the value of another being. Recognizing humanness in ourselves and others enables us to deal with our contradictions and prejudices, making us more loving and accepting of others.

As you place **divine** on the altar, visualize the part of yourself that is sacred and divine.

I know that I am divine and deserving of
all that is good.

"i found god in myself / & i loved her / i loved her fiercely."
Ntozake Shange, *For Colored Girls Who Have Considered Suicide
When the Rainbow Is Enuf* (1975)

Dream

When was the last time you allowed yourself the luxury of daydreaming? Dreams make realities. Dreaming the impossible is a wonderful way to make unbelievable things happen. But many of us have become so turned off to the magic of life that we don't take time to dream the way we used to. It is okay to picture yourself having things that you deserve, accomplishing goals, and being the person you want to be.

Dreaming keeps us alive, it keeps us in touch with the past and the future. We stand on the shoulders of our dreaming ancestors. We learn of our grandparents' dreams for their children to have a life better than theirs. Their dreams become our hope for the future. We must remember to acknowledge that privileges we take for granted existed, at one time, only in our ancestors' imaginations.

Dreaming is a private affair, something we can do without anyone else knowing. Your dream can be a secret desire or an ambitious plan involving many people. The important thing is to visualize your dream daily and spend some time making it happen.

Take time to dream . . . it is a necessary activity for living.

As you place **dream** on the altar, recall a dream that you haven't thought about for a long time.

I will paint my dreams upon the world, knowing that they create my realities.

"The least I can say for myself is that I forcefully created for myself, under extremely hostile conditions, my ideal life. I took an obscure and almost unknown village in the Southern African bush and made it my own hallowed ground. Here, in the steadiness and peace of my own world, I could dream dreams a little ahead of the somewhat vicious clamor of revolution and the horrible stench of evil social systems."

Bessie Head

Empowerment

When we give ourselves permission to be powerful, we give authority to others to be powerful. When we get power, we also have the responsibility to share that power with others. A person's process of empowerment is ignited by action, words, or insights that she identifies as growth-producing.

We can turn life experiences into empowering events. While working at Birthplace, I noticed that women would apologize for making loud noises during birth when, in fact, they were not that loud. I figured out that when women are fully dilated, their hearing is sensitive and intensified, so I decided to take advantage of this. Between contractions, I would get in their ear and say, "You are so powerful, you are magnificent, you are doing such a good job." The next contraction was met with renewed strength. But the most interesting part is that women would tell me that for years after their labor experience they could still hear my voice in their heads. It gave them a source of power and strength that they could tap into, especially on bad days.

It is so easy and gratifying to give empowering messages. Power is not to be feared, but claimed, shared, and celebrated.

Place **empowerment** on the altar and feel your strength, wisdom, and generosity.

I will share my power knowing I will be fulfilled.

"Self-definition is intimately linked with empowerment."
Judy Scales-Trent, Associate Professor of Law and Jurisprudence,
SUNY-Buffalo, School of Law

Free Spirit

Many times we refer to a person as "strange" or "eccentric" when she is simply different. I ask that you reexamine your perspective and think of such a person as a "free spirit." The poem "When I Am an Old Woman I Shall Wear Purple," by Jenny Joseph is about giving oneself permission to wear a color that is associated with free spirits. Making a decision to live your life the way you want is a powerful act. Give yourself permission to do as you please as long as it does not infringe upon the rights of others.

For many years I lived my life worrying about what others thought about me. I worried about what they might say about the way I dressed, the company I kept, or where I went. I spent far too much time putting the opinions of others ahead of my own thoughts, desires, or wishes. In 1974 I traveled to New York

City and saw Black women with their hair close-cropped. I fell in love with that style, and wanted it for myself. It took me a couple of months to get my nerve to do it. I kept thinking of my family and friends who would disapprove, who would say, "What woman would cut her hair that short?"

When I finally cut my hair, some folks liked it and some didn't, but I was most amazed at the people who acted like it never happened. This was a real turning point for me. I was elated that I was able to stop thinking about what others thought, and start listening to and following my own heart.

Now is the time to start pleasing ourselves. When I stopped worrying about others so much I felt free to explore my inner self and my outer world. Thinking of being eccentric as being free to express oneself is a positive affirmation of inner feelings and desires.

As you place **free spirit** on the altar, think of something you secretly want to do but haven't done yet.

I am giving myself permission to explore
avenues of expression.

"I love different folks."
Eleanor H. Porter, *Pollyanna* (1913)

Faith

My mother went to Bethune-Cookman College while Mary McLeod Bethune was alive and very visible on the campus. I spent many days on that campus attending programs, going to football games, and watching parades. I met Mrs. Bethune several times, and on one occasion she took my small hand in hers, covered it with the other hand, and asked me, "Are you planning to come to Cookman?" I told her of my plans to attend Talladega College. She said, "Fine, it is important that you go somewhere." I have always remembered this as a moment when greatness touched me. She was a very charismatic, highly respected woman, full of faith and determination.

Faith is knowing within yourself that a possibility can become a reality. Mary McLeod Bethune embodied faith. She believed in the possibility of founding a college for Blacks, and starting with nothing more than ten dollars, five students, and two orange crates, she succeeded. Her legacy still inspires.

Mrs. Bethune died during my senior year in high school and we attended her funeral, sitting in the overflow area outside Faith Chapel. This strong woman served as a great role model for us during the times of severe segregation in the Deep South. It was affirming to see her picture on the cover of magazines and articles about her talks with President Franklin Delano Roosevelt and the respectful relationship she had with Eleanor Roosevelt. Mrs. Bethune had faith that the people of the United States would rise up against segregation and bigotry.

Several years ago I visited Bethune-Cookman College's campus and I could still feel her presence. I toured her home, which embodied the spirit of a woman who founded not only a college but several organizations, and challenged us all to examine our social responsibilities. She was truly a giant in all senses of the word.

Mrs. Bethune's spirit lives on inside me. She is among a group of wise ancestors I reach out to when I feel especially challenged. I put together a committee of Mary Bethune, Sojourner Truth, Harriet Tubman, and one or two others, tell them my problem, ask for their help in solving it, and go to sleep. I awake full of ideas and direction.

As you place **faith** on the altar, feel its strength and inner power.

I have faith in myself and I know the universe will respond positively.

"Faith is the first factor in a life devoted to service. Without faith, nothing is possible. With it, nothing is impossible."
Mary McLeod Bethune

Family

How many times have we observed habits of our mothers and said, "I don't want to be like that." Well, guess what, many of us will end up with a lot of our mother's habits and mannerisms. I imagine most mothers felt the same way about their mothers. I would hear myself telling my young children the same words my mother said to me, "Byllye, clean your room, it looks like the wreck of the *Hesperus.*" Now, I had no idea what the wreck of the *Hesperus* was, but I knew my room was a mess and this was my last warning. This command will, of course, be taken to the next generation. There is an invisible golden thread that weaves our generations together. Actions and words that feel so right and seem to come from nowhere, probably came to us lovingly across several generations.

We pass along eating habits, mannerisms, family rituals, and personal experiences. For example, all the women in a family experience the first menstruation. We must make a conscious effort so that this introduction to womanhood is a good experience, answering questions honestly and truthfully, creating a positive space for sharing information. Shared experience gives us an opportunity for special bonding and acknowledging that special day with the creation of a ritual welcoming our daughters to womanhood. This first experience is one that is remembered by all women, so create something memorable and sacred to be passed on to future generations of women in your family.

I recently started talking to my mother every day and we take delight in sharing important and unimportant events of our day. I am learning so much about my mother: her daily activities, her past life, her dreams, and her future plans. She continues to learn about me and my life. This daily connection is a part of my life that I eagerly look forward to and is a gift to both of us.

As we increase our connections to family members we learn a lot about ourselves and one another.

As you place **family** on the altar, think of the ways in which you are connected to the past and the future.

I love and affirm the parts of me that span
the generations.

*"What families have in common the world around is that they are the place
where people learn who they are and how to be that way."*
Jean Illsley Clarke, *Self-Esteem: A Family Affair* (1978)

Fatigue

We are a nation of tired people. We have many labor-saving devices that make us work faster and harder. Work requests are made quicker by fax machines, e-mail, and voice mail. We are running as fast as we can to keep up. Workers who are still on the job after a company downsizes don't know whether they are lucky or not since they are often doing the work of several people. We can't stop technological advances, but we can set some boundaries for ourselves.

It is important that we build in time for ourselves, to do nothing, to relax. We need to get a good night's sleep, giving the body the amount it needs. I need eight hours of sleep on a good mattress in order to feel refreshed in the morning. On less sleep I feel tired, have a hard time paying attention, suffer from irritability, and am less productive.

Walking is one of the most effective exercises, providing needed physical activity and relaxation. Walk for wellness heals all parts of the body. Try listening to music that is soothing, that speaks to your soul and spirit. Sometimes the nightly news is so depressing I give myself permission to not listen every evening. We don't need too many negative images in our minds. Fill yourself up with good news, information that provides energy and nourishment. Go to see a nonviolent movie or, better still, rent an old movie that you know will inspire and stimulate you.

We must create spaces where we can retreat from daily stresses and create balance in our lives. Be good to yourself, and you will prevent physical and spiritual fatigue.

As you place **fatigue** on the altar, make a commitment to participate in one stress-relieving activity today.

I am worthy of not feeling fatigued most of my life.
I deserve rest and rejuvenation.

"*Then, I pillowed myself in goodness and slept righteously.*"
Maya Angelou, *All God's Children Need Traveling Shoes* (1986)

Fresh Air

I like to walk in the mornings, I find that it is easy to breathe in the fresh morning air as it fills and replenishes my lungs and heart. The trees gently greet me as the soft cool breezes help cleanse my mind. The birds' songs provide a melody of healing.

We can take a lesson from nature and freshen the air around us indoors as well. The care and love we give to plants return to us cleaner air and aesthetic beauty. It is also necessary to cleanse the air of negative thoughts and energy that pollute our reality. Plan to spend some time each day breathing fresh air.

Feel and deeply breathe **fresh air** as you place this word on the altar.

I will breathe deeply and enjoy the fresh air around me.

"Nature has been for me, for as long as I can remember, a source of solace, inspiration, adventure, and delight; a home, a teacher, a companion."

Lorraine Anderson, *Sisters of Earth* (1991)

Friendship

Friends tend to mirror parts of ourselves. I have a dear friend, Jill, of thirty years and, while we don't talk daily, whenever we talk we are back in our usual warm, loving space. It is so comforting to know that place is always available to me. Positive people in our lives make life worthwhile. Surround yourself with positive people whose energy is empowering, full of growth and support.

Susan L. Taylor reminds us in her book *In the Spirit* to be careful how we choose our friends because negative people do not deserve to have a front row seat in our lives. We should love these friends from a distance. Some people have a critical view of life, always seeing the glass half empty. Often they care a lot and want the best, but their negative approach can create anxiety and defensiveness in others and make them less desirable to be around. We must continue to love them from afar and hope they will change their perspective on life.

After my husband died, my friends became a part of my loving family. We shared child care, vacations, and illnesses, and weathered good and bad times. They became my extended family by being caring uncles and aunts who took a lot of the pressure off me. We created our village of support, making life easier and more fulfilling for all of us. We rejoice in the success of our children and worry about their challenges. Friends are family created from a desire and commitment to be together.

Our lives are enriched by our friends. They help us make it through the hard times and celebrate the good times.

As you place **friendship** on the altar, think about your closest friend, and whisper "I love you" in her ear.

I am deserving of having positive friends. I will surround myself with their presence.

"If I don't have friends, then I ain't got nothin'."
Billie Holiday

Gift

The universe gives us gifts every day. Sometimes we are blessed with a gift as big as the sky and other times we receive gifts as subtle as a gentle breeze. At first, I really didn't believe I would get a gift every day; I would have been satisfied with once a week. And yet, what a pleasant surprise it is to know my gift for each day comes uniquely wrapped, with its own spirit and energy.

Knowing that you will receive a gift means paying attention to your interactions, the offerings of nature, the smile of a child, or the beauty of a butterfly. Receiving gifts means opening your heart and senses to endless possibilities. One of the last things I do before I fall asleep is to note my gift for that day. Sometimes it is pleasant thoughts about friends and loved ones. Other times it is a sunset, a new flower bloom, or a great conversation I had with someone.

Gifts are easy to give to others. Sometimes speaking and smiling at people you don't normally interact with brings cheer. Go ahead and give a compliment to a sister who is dressed to the nines. Tell her she looks good—your comment might just make her day.

We are privileged to be alive and to be members of the human race. We live in a beautiful world, with glorious sunrises and -sets, oceans blue and roaring, and a sky that paints us in the universe. Thank the Creator for allowing you to wake up every morning in this grand and glorious place.

Recall your **gift** for today and place it on your altar.

I open myself to giving and receiving the gifts of the universe.

"To those leaning on the sustaining infinite, today is big with blessings."
Mary Baker Eddy, *Science and Health* (1875)

Guidance

Often I am asked by caring friends, "What do you do when you get stuck?" What I do is ask for help. I turn to a trusted friend or I meditate and take long walks. I pray more than usual.

Sometimes I turn to a book of inspirational readings entitled *A Guide for the Advanced Soul: A Book of Insight*, by Susan Hayward. This is an amazing book. You hold a problem in your mind, open the book to any page, and there you will find your answer. Sometimes I consult it more than once about the same issue, and the message of the passage remains the same. This book provides me with wisdom and guidance. Once I lost my passport I searched everywhere and finally decided to consult the book; and the passage instructed me to be like a very small joyous child, living gloriously in the ever-present now without a single worry or concern about even the next moment of time. I thought about these words for over an hour and figured out that a child would be close to the floor, got down on my hands and knees and located it between the head of my bed and the wall. It was the most incredible thing. Many of my friends have consulted this book and received remarkable guidance.

We receive guidance from many places in the environment. Some we hear immediately and some we hear later and some we wish we had never heard. Guidance is for receiving and giving; this exchange produces growth.

As you place **guidance** on the altar, understand that nothing is by chance.

I am open to the guidance of the universe.

"Every moment of your life is infinitely creative and the universe is endlessly bountiful. Just put forth a clear enough request, and everything your heart desires must come to you."

Shakti Gawain, *Creative Visualization* (1978)

Happiness

Are you happy? When was the last time you felt genuinely happy? Are you happy in your present relationship, with your job, about the place where you live? Do you know what makes you happy? Was there ever a time when you felt you were happy—you know—sitting on top of the world? Sometimes we are afraid to ask these questions, and we are equally afraid of the answers. It is difficult to talk about being happy for fear that it will disappear just as it magically appeared in our life. That's why we knock on wood.

Happiness is one of those supreme feelings that can be appreciated because we have unhappy times. And, quite frankly, if we were happy all of the time life would be boring. However, we would be happy with a little more of this type of boredom. Seek happiness. It belongs to you.

We make our own happiness and we all deserve to have it in quantity. Make it a priority to participate in activities that will lift your spirits, and be around people who have positive attitudes. Let yourself have fun. It really is all right and it is necessary for wellness. If you can't make yourself happy, who do you think can? It starts first on the inside and flows outward. So start thinking happy thoughts so you can be happy. If you are already happy, cherish your good fortune. Happiness is a precious gift.

As you place **happiness** on the altar, imagine yourself in a blessed state.

> I am a child of the universe. I deserve and accept happiness.

"When one door of happiness closes another opens; but often we look so long at the closed door that we do not see the one which has been opened for us."
Helen Keller, *We Bereaved* (1929)

Healing

There are many ways to heal. Tears and laughter are important parts of the healing process. When we connect to our painful feelings from past hurts, this pain causes us to cry, and we begin to heal. Laughing about something that was embarrassing or anxiety-provoking in the past provides a feeling of relief. It is baggage that can be discarded because it has been dealt with and your perspective on the issue has changed.

Another way of healing is the sharing of stories. In the early days of the women's movement, this was called consciousness-raising. It simply meant sharing experiences with others, often of events and feelings we had never shared before. This sharing made women aware of their common experiences. The more women talked about their relationships with their families, school experiences, love life, and society in general, the better they felt.

On a physical level many of us have participated in charting our own course of wellness. Our health care regimes may include herbs, faith, and prayer. Sometimes all we have is our faith, which makes us aware of our vulnerabilities and strengthens our spirit. As we share with others, we offer them the power of our healing experiences.

As you put **healing** on the altar, recall one of your healing stories, and think of who could benefit from hearing it at the right time.

I have the power within myself to contribute to
my personal healing.

*"I got well by talking. Death could not get a word in edgewise,
grew discouraged, and traveled on."*
Louise Erdrich, *Tracks* (1988)

Healing Waters

Few experiences can top the feeling of sinking into a warm tub of bubbles. Healing waters create a sanctuary where one can escape the stress and responsibilities of the world. A tub is a place to be rid of clothes and cares—to let go and watch each bubble capture our worries and burst into forgetfulness. A bubble bath cleanses the spirit and relaxes the mind into a state of solitude. Time alone is a healing gift to the soul. The gift of water, air, soap, and time allows us to heal and relieve our psyche and soul.

The healing magic of a bubble bath works best if taken often. Schedule yourself an appointment to indulge in the tub. This is what wellness is all about. If you have children, you will be modeling for them a healthy way to relieve stress and helping them learn that it is okay to take time for oneself.

As you put **healing waters** on the altar, visualize yourself in a tub
of soothing bubbles.

I recognize the stress and tension in my body
and I will release it.

*"A hot bath! How exquisite a vespertine pleasure, how luxurious,
fervid and flagrant a consolation for the rigors, the austerities,
the renunciations of the day."*
Rose Macaulay, *Personal Pleasures* (1936)

Health

Gather your courage and get your yearly physical checkup. We are all so scared that the doctors will find something, namely cancer. This six-letter word keeps many of us from getting our Pap smears, even though cervical cancer can be cured if detected early. It takes courage to get a mammogram, even though we know that it does not hurt and is not that unpleasant. Get a Pap smear, pelvic and breast exams, blood pressure and urine tests yearly.

We must be brave and more honest when we talk to others about our illnesses and maladies. Feelings of shame and embarrassment have kept us silent. But if we take the risk to share, we are giving a gift to ourselves and the listener. I remember a sister standing up at a National Black Women's Health Project meeting and saying, "I must share with you. I have a lump in my breast. I'm scared and I need someone to go with me to the doctor." About fifty hands went up around the room.

Since asking for help is hard for some of us to do, start giving support to women as birthday gifts. Ask the sister if she has had her yearly exam, and then ask if she needs some support. If she does, go with her for the appointment and then take her out to lunch afterward. We can share our courageous behavior with each other in powerful, life-saving ways. The courage to heal often starts with the courage to be honest and open yourself to the blessings of the universe.

As you put **health** on the altar, recognize the importance of your health and well-being.

I am deserving of optimal health, and I will take care of myself.

"It is more blessed to give than to receive, so give to yourself as much as you can as often as you can."

LaVerne Porter-Wheatley Perry, Clinical Psychologist

Heart

When the sisters of the National Black Women's Health Project were asked to talk personally about cardiovascular disease, they talked about issues that caused their hearts to hurt. The immediate association with heart disease was emotional pain. These women were not talking about the regular ups and downs of life—they expected life to have joys and sorrows. They were talking about hardships that come from twisted and penetrating racism.

Women immediately started talking about how difficult it is to rear sons. They discussed how African American boys grow up so close to crime, and they see it almost daily in the lives of their peers. It is so easy for these boys to be in the wrong place at the wrong time. Society provides constant negative feedback in conscious and unconscious ways. One woman said that if you want to see the impact of society on our health, look at the criminal justice system, go to court, see who is on trial and who is crying out in pain. We live in a country with confused priorities. We readily spend $50,000 a year to keep a person in jail forever, but we won't give money for him or her to go to college for four years. Once a person is jailed, there is little or no attempt at rehabilitation or at providing the tools and support to help him or her become functioning members of society.

This is all difficult to process when we know that all human beings were born good and whole. We all come into the world with good hearts, we are good-hearted at the center of our being. The fortunes and misfortunes of our experiences shape our very being and form our perspective and life outcome. Our hearts hurt from unhealed pain of incidents that erode our self-esteem, from unresolved interactions and anger turned inward. When we internalize the oppression heaped on us by others, our hearts become so heavy the load of carrying it seems unbearable.

Deep inside we must become aware that we deserve to have the very best that life has to offer. We must seek to claim our right to this blessing of the universe. It is important to face the issues we are afraid of; they contain a source of power that is needed for growth. As we recognize internalized oppression and start to unhook from this thinking and actions, we gain strength to heal our hearts and mend our souls. We were not put here on earth to be abused by anyone and we don't have to take it!

As you put **heart** on your altar, claim your power and use it for self-healing.

I know that my heart center is good and free of pain. I will work to connect with its spirit within.

"There is much pain that is quite noiseless; and vibrations that make human agonies are often a mere whisper in the roar of hurrying existence."
George Eliot, *Felix Holt, the Radical* (1866)

Heaven

Life's challenges can cause some of us to dream about escaping to heaven. We want our existence to continue in a wonderful place where all is peaceful and bountiful. Sunday school lessons always made me think of heaven as a place high above the clouds, filled with spirits that live eternally without a worry. We had a Bible school teacher who reinforced this notion with her felt board of biblical characters and heavenly scenes.

At age twenty, when my grandfather died, I started to wonder, "What happens to people when they die?" I knew that if there was a heaven, then my grandfather had to be there. In my eyes, he was as good as gold. I remember his words to my husband on my wedding day. He said, "Wesley, treat this woman with respect. If you even think about raising your hand to strike her, bring her back home to her parents where she is loved and respected. She is your wife, not your property." Yes, he was as good as gold. Heaven becomes real when we are faced with the death of a loved one.

As I got older, I learned more about the stages of dying as well as the powerful lessons of near-death experiences. My concept of heaven was radically altered. Heaven, I came to believe, might be all around us—filling up the in-between spaces and creating eternal time. How else can we explain miracles, or people who see and communicate with the dead? I find great comfort in knowing that in a spirit form or as an angel we can experience the wonders of this great world. This helps me realize that God exists in all of us—that we each have a unique goodness given to us by the Creator. This makes the earth a place for physical existence and a place for the spirits to reside.

In my mind, we need to rethink the concept of heaven on earth. It just might be possible for them both to exist in the same place—not heaven in the clouds, but heaven in your house, in your yard, on the rooftops, at work, on the playground, and everywhere.

As you place **heaven** on the altar, think about the spiritual energy that surrounds you.

I am a part of heaven. I claim heaven as a calm, peaceful place for myself.

"Heaven is neither a place nor a time."
Florence Nightingale

Honesty

As children we start learning about honesty when we get caught in lies, try to trick adults, or just are disobedient. I had a blue gingham plaid dress that was gathered at the waist, and I loved that dress. It was one of my Sunday dresses, which meant it was not to be worn to school. One day I was sneaky and wore it to school, which just happened to be the day that some stupid boy, trying to catch me, grabbed me by the skirt and tore the dress at the waist. When I got home, I hid the dress in the back of the closet, and told my mother I could not find it. When she found it she disciplined me, but the real pain was in her disappointment at my being disobedient and dishonest.

To thine own self be true. Most of the time these "truths" are the most difficult. We know what we want and like, but do we risk being honest all of the time? This, we fear, could lead to disapproval or the loss of friends. Some of us don't have the time to be honest—we are moving so fast in the world that there is no time to explain or make others understand the truth. Is this loss of integrity worth the gains of dishonesty? Are there really situations that make it okay to tell a little harmless lie?

As we become more spiritually in tune with ourselves, we feel less need to be dishonest. We must trust our own honest responses and be satisfied with knowing that we did the right thing, not the most acceptable thing. Practicing honesty is a lifetime process that keeps us present and filled with hope knowing that there will be a future.

When you place **honesty** on the altar, know that inner honesty is foremost and sacred.

I will acknowledge truths in myself and speak truths to my world today.

"You never find yourself until you face the truth."
Pearl Bailey, *The Raw Pearl* (1968)

Hugs

It's interesting to watch people hug each other. Some hug with an arched back and little pats on the back with their fingertips, while others take you into their arms and give you a good smashing embrace. No matter how you do it, people will know if you're a hugger. It's as if they can tell by the energy they feel around you when you hear them say with outstretched arms "I just need a hug."

Arms and hugging are universal icebreakers. A warm hug makes a person feel comfortable in a short time, especially if he or she was hugged to death as a child by family members. Many of us had an aunt or cousin with well-endowed bosoms who taught us what hugging is. Hugs can stop tears or make a place for them if needed. Hugs can show warmth and melt icy feelings. A hug is a gift.

We hug a lot in the National Black Women's Health Project; it makes us feel good to touch our sisters. Hugs caress our spirits and comfort our souls.

When you place **hug** on the altar, wrap yourself in a warm embrace.

I love myself, and I feel my arms caressing me.

"She who raises her arms will be embraced."
Yoruba proverb

Imagination

A child's laugh reflects the magic of imagination. When we are children, our minds are free and clear and can focus on the moment. Children's psyches are not loaded with past experiences and fears. Purity and innocence allow us to travel easily to unknown places in our minds. These journeys show us that all things are possible.

We know that childhood is fleeting, and childish behavior is unacceptable in adults. Yet we can learn to explore the vastness of our imagination. Just as we did in childhood. We can access our dreams when we permit them to emerge. Work hard to keep your imagination alive; it is one of your sources of power and inspiration.

Jump-start your imagination by removing the barriers that limit your thoughts. Words like "can't" and "should" have no place in your imagination. Dreaming keeps your mind open to new ideas and possibilities.

As you place **imagination** on the altar, relax, allow your mind to open up to a new, unexplored space in the universe.

I am blessed and I will encourage my imagination to take me on an unexplored journey in the universe.

"Indigo, I don't want to hear another word about it, do you understand me. I'm not setting the table with my Sunday china for fifteen dolls who got their period today."

Ntozake Shange, *Sassafras, Cypress & Indigo* (1982)

Inspiration

When was the last time you felt inspired? Was it was a good book that made you feel so powerful that you just couldn't get enough of it or put it down? Was it a Sunday morning sermon?

My work as an activist has been inspired. In 1983, we convened the First National Conference on Black Women's Health Issues at Spelman College. The words of Fannie Lou Hamer—"I'm Sick and Tired of Being Sick and Tired"—was the theme that echoed the feelings of the two thousand women who attended. We broke the conspiracy of silence about our health. We talked in ways we had never talked before. We laughed, cried, celebrated, and made a commitment to changing our lives—we were inspired.

I am also inspired by the human spirit: the child who returns a wallet full of cash, when she would love to buy sneakers; the person who takes meals to homebound seniors; the child who has manners. I am inspired when I hear Dr. King's speeches or Sojourner Truth's "Ain't I a Woman?" We can live with respect and harmony. These acts and words make us know that we are human and deserve respect and honor. We can be moved by hearing inspiring stories about the struggles of our sisters. We learn and grow from hearing of the ways in which they have been able to survive odds that seem insurmountable. Inspiration motivates us to do many things and act in new ways.

As you put **inspiration** on the altar, plan on attending a motivating event.

Inspiration is divine and it is mine to experience.

"Let a new earth rise. Let another world be born. Let a bloody peace be written in the sky. Let a second generation full of courage issue forth; let a people loving freedom come to growth."

Margaret Walker

Integrity

On my first trip to Amsterdam to attend a conference, I had the pleasure of visiting a Dutch family. Our hostess shared with us all the cultural benefits of living in Amsterdam: the museums, the efficient transportation system, accessible health care delivery, the opera, theaters, etc. With great pride, she showed us her museum pass, which, for a nominal fee, admitted her to all of the museums.

At one point in the conversation I asked her what she did for a living. She said, "I work as a cleaner at the airport and I love my job." I was puzzled by this because I had always thought people who performed cleaning jobs hated their work. This interaction made me think about this type of work differently.

How many of us enter a bathroom that is neat and clean and take it for granted? We only appreciate a clean bathroom when we encounter a dirty one. But someone has to have a sense of integrity to make sure the job is done, and done well. We call it meeting basic standards, but who makes sure they are met? Integrity means being honest and understanding the importance of each job to the well-being of society. Teachers, reporters, doctors, train operators, fast food service workers—we all contribute to a civilized and orderly society.

As you place **integrity** on the altar, make a promise to recognize and appreciate workers who contribute to your well-being.

I live with integrity and I respect the
integrity of others.

"Remember always that you have not only the right to be an individual, you have an obligation to be one. You cannot make any useful contribution in life unless you do this."

Eleanor Roosevelt

Joy

Absolute joy is the kind of joy that you feel all over your body. How often is it that we feel joy that is so intense that your body can hardly stand it? Pure joy brings us great delight that turns the world on around us and makes us wish we could remain suspended in its grasp forever.

Children present us with joyful experiences: seeing a newborn baby or hearing a child's first words, steps, and discoveries. These experiences bring delight and stay in our memories to be recalled and enjoyed later.

Remember to celebrate joyous occasions: they nourish our souls and spirits. Joy keeps us looking forward to the future while we remain in touch with the past. It links us across generations and contributes to our collective memories. Joy is everlasting. We could not survive as a people without joy.

As you place **joy** on the altar, allow your mind to recall the last time you felt joy deep inside.

I am worthy of having joy in my life, I welcome it and will be nourished by the experience.

"The sharing of joy, whether physical, emotional, psychic or intellectual, forms a bridge between the sharers which can be the basis for understanding much of what is not shared between them, and lessens the threat of their difference."

Audre Lorde, *Uses of the Erotic* (1978)

Kindness

There was a tradition in the Black community that involved extraordinary acts of kindness. It was the tradition of receiving a "gift child." If a family or a single young woman fell on hard times and was unable to care for a child, caring adults would take the child, rear it, and treat it as their own. It was viewed as a gift to the accepting family, although I always thought of the accepting family as giving a supreme gift to the child and her family. It was a beautiful act of kindness and was a tradition in our community.

My mother endured a long hospitalization several years ago that required her friends and family to spend a lot of time at the hospital. In addition to decorating her room, we became friends with all of the staff, which helped to personalize her care. Upon her discharge, we threw a party for the staff and selected hospital

administrators. They were overwhelmed, surprised, and appreciative. No one had ever validated them that way before. It was a
small thing for us to do, and it meant so much to them.

If we are able to stretch a little every day and commit a kind
act, that stretching will enable us to melt away negativity. Acts of
kindness make our day. Acts of kindness affirm that we are
human and a part of a caring universe.

Place **kindness** on your altar with great care.

I will notice acts of kindness given to me and I will
reward myself by being kind to others.

KINDNESS CURES
(Sign at a nursing home in Falmouth, Massachusetts)

Kisses

Very few things that can top the expressions of love embodied in a kiss. A magical kiss leaves a lasting imprint on one's body and soul.

A kiss is often the first expression of intimacy. The first step to falling in love. A special magical space that we delight in entering. Kisses are erotic when they enable us to share intimate moments. A kiss is the blending of our spirits and a sinking into a unified oneness.

Kisses can signal the beginning of a relationship. Kissing is the easiest part of becoming a couple; the work is in making the relationship last.

We kiss our children, our parents, our friends. It can be one of our most loving actions. When we are generous with our love, it enables us to receive love.

As you put **kisses** on the altar, vividly remember a great kiss you've had.

I am worthy of all of the warmth that a kiss brings;
I am open to its generosity.

"Life is short, and it's up to you to make it sweet."
Sadie Delaney, *Having Our Say* (1993)

Laughter

When I was twelve years old, a friend and I went to visit my Aunt Gert and my cousin in Albany, Georgia. We were playing hopscotch in the backyard, on the sun-baked red Georgia clay. I couldn't stop hopping and landed in a patch of sand spurs. I laughed so hard I wet my pants, and the urine stain stayed on the Georgia clay for years to come. My cousin and I would return to the spot and relive that day, and laugh.

Take a moment and remember a funny incident from your childhood. It feels so good to laugh until water flows from your eyes. A good storyteller can make a dull party lively, just by making people laugh. We naturally like to be around people who can make us laugh.

Laughter sounds the same in all languages. Laughter provides a universal way for us to share common experiences without translation. I participated in a workshop led by a Navajo who taught us the importance of laughter in reducing stress. Within minutes, he had us all cracking up at his jokes. Sometimes we laughed because he was laughing, and sometimes we looked at each other and laughed, not knowing or caring why. An interesting bond developed when we laughed together for the five straight hours of the workshop, pausing only to catch our breath. Laughter is good medicine. Try to have a good laugh at least once a day. If there is nothing to laugh about, think about the last time you cracked up, and let out a good one.

As you place **laughter** on the altar, laugh out loud.

I will enjoy the healing power of laughter.

"Laughing stirs up the blood, expands the chest, electrifies the nerves, clears away the cobwebs from the brain, and gives the whole system a cleansing rehabilitation."

Anonymous

Love

There's nothing like falling in love! It has to be one of the best feelings. I remember the last time I fell in love, I was so happy I got down on my knees and thanked the Lord for allowing me to have this special feeling just one more time. When I'm in love, the world is such a good place and all problems are either funny or solvable.

Love is the warmth we felt when we gazed into our mamas' eyes while she took care of us, loving us so much. She kissed our little fat feet and our smooth bottoms. Daddies loved us with a deeper voice, tossed us around carefully like a sack of potatoes, overprotected us, made us feel love in a different way. As grown women, we love others, too—our husbands, our lovers, our children, our relations, and our global family.

In the midst of all of this, sometimes we forget to love ourselves, even while we love everyone who needs it and whomever our arms will go around. We forget about the self-love that we need to keep going. We have elevated taking care of others at our own expense to a high level. It is always wise to remember that others will survive even if we are not there taking care of them. I found out that I feel so much better when I take an hour a day, just to take care of me and love myself. It keeps me from feeling so put upon by everything and everybody and helps me get through the day. By taking my hour early in the morning, I feel like I get my love first and I get it when I am at my best.

Love is so powerful. When we fail to take care of ourselves, we rob ourselves of additional power. We all know that when we are able to love and take care of ourselves, we are better able to love others. Self-love means we know that there is no one who can fill all of our needs and that self-love can fill in all of the creases and crevices. When we are full of inner love, it's easy for our love to spill over to others.

Love your very being and the world will open up with wonderful possibilities. Love yourself unconditionally. We might not like all of the things we do, the words we say, or how we behave, but we must love ourselves. As we share love in the world, the more love we receive.

As you place **love** on the altar, think about the ways in which you can love yourself more fully.

I am worthy of my radiant love. I will love myself
and rejoice in my spirit.

"We love because it is the only true adventure."
Nikki Giovanni, *Reader's Digest* (1982)

Mommy

"Mommy" is the softer side of motherhood. When we say, "I want my Mommy," we are speaking about the warm/soft/cuddly/take care of me/be there for me always mother. When girls and women say they want to be a mother, rocking a baby to sleep, they are hugging away disappointment, or kissing the pain out of the bruise. They are thinking of those tender moments when it feels good being needed and we enjoy the giving.

We must be both Mommy and Mother. We must be there when we are tired and when our child has been crying nonstop for several hours in the middle of the night. When children get angry and throw a tantrum or graduate to "I hate you" to express their anger, we must stay by them. Put the Mommy side away momentarily, so that this behavior can be dealt with.

All mothers can remember the difficult times of mothering, but most of us get great pleasure from thinking about the cuddly, comforting times. There are few thoughts more pleasurable than remembering cute sayings, a kiss that seemingly came from no-where but was right on time, a bunch of flowers clutched in tiny fingers. These are the moments that give us lasting memories and let us know that life is wonderful in its simplicity.

As you place **Mommy** on the altar, feel her arms around you, feel her kissing you gently all over your face.

I claim the part of me that is soft, warm, and cuddly. I am one of the Mommies of the universe.

"Who ran to help me when I fell, / And would some pretty story tell, / Or kiss the place to make it well? / My mother."
Ann Taylor, "My Mother" (1804)

Moon Set

One early morning I drove from Los Angeles to Santa Barbara and I had the pleasure of watching the moon set over the Pacific Ocean. As I watched the moon's subdued light shimmering over the sea, I found myself releasing a lot of stress. It was easy for me to release my thoughts and concentrate on the present, absorbing the reflection of the moon, the clarity of the sea, and the beauty of the scenery.

The second gift I received that day was the beautiful landscape that the sky creates at daybreak. While I think of myself as an early riser, this is not an experience that I can recall having before, especially seaside. I felt my body relax further as I surrendered myself completely to my surroundings.

Despite the early hour when I arrived at my destination, I

realized that my moon set and daybreak ride helped me to arrive energized and ready to work.

As you place **moon set** on the altar, make a commitment to watch the moon.

I know the universe provides me with opportunities to rejuvenate my spirit; I will draw upon them.

"The astronomers tell us that other planets are gifted with two-four-even nine lavish moons. Imagine the romantic possibilities of nine moons."
Edna Ferber, *A Kind of Magic* (1963)

Mother

Mother is a word that embraces many roles and many kinds of love. We think of Mother Earth, and the motherland, as our foundation, our place of origin. A motherhouse is a spiritual home, and a mother lode supplies us with energy and resources. All of what this word means is also tied up in our expectations and need of mothers. This word contains the words "other" and "her." We have other mothers who take care of us at different times and love us in different ways. Other mothers make up the important village that it takes to raise a child—maybe a teacher, an aunt, or the woman whose house the kids hang out in.

I love my mother. She has been the most consistent person in my life, even when my personal decisions have challenged her beliefs and attitudes. It has always been clear that she loves me. Her intense and supportive love for me has helped me cross many bridges safely and with confidence. She is the person I admire and appreciate the most. Thank you, Mother dear, for being a dear mother.

As you place **mother** on the altar, take a moment and think about the mothers in your life.

I am full of my mother's love, which comforts me.

"Next to God we are indebted to women, first for life itself, and then for making it worth living."
Mary McLeod Bethune

Nourishment

You need to feed and nourish yourself: your mind, your soul, your heart, and your body. When you give and give with little return, you begin to function like an empty well. Take responsibility for creating a wellspring of nourishment that will replenish you and make you feel whole again.

There are twenty-four hours in each day and you are certainly worthy of having one of them, just for you. Initially, hold a family meeting, explain that you will be taking one hour each day for yourself, alone. Be sure to stress *alone*. Give your family emergency telephone numbers so they can call someone else to meet their pressing needs during *your* hour. Take your hour and engage in an activity that relaxes you, like taking a walk, or soaking in the tub for an hour, or going into your bedroom, locking the door, taking off your clothes, and getting into bed. You deserve this time and space.

Place **nourishment** on the altar, knowing that you will take care of yourself.

I will take an hour a day to take care of myself.

"It's essential that we understand that taking care of the planet will be done as we take care of ourselves."
Alice Walker

Passion

Before I became involved with the women's health movement, I didn't feel passionate about anything political. I was a working mother and a special education teacher, but I still didn't feel fulfilled. I took sewing and upholstery classes at the community college trying to keep from being bored to death. When I discovered the women's health movement and became passionate about it, my work became more meaningful and gratifying. Passion is a great motivator; many things are accomplished in the throes of passion.

Many things make us feel passionate, whether it be work, a hobby, a political issue, or love. Passions are consuming. Passion takes us on a sweet journey, to a place where we can block out almost everything and focus on the task with intensity. This exciting journey is one that is filled with new learning and great joy.

The color of passion is red, full of warm feelings, bursting with love and radiant energy. Passionate feelings for a loved one fill our bodies with eroticism that makes us understand the true meaning of pleasure. We wish we could remain arrested in this magical state forever.

As you tenderly lay **passion** on your altar, feel its warmth throughout your body.

I cherish my moments of passion.

"Passion is our ground, our island—do others exist?"
Eudora Welty, "Circe," *The Bride of Innisfallen* (1955)

Perseverance

There are times when life seems difficult, the way seems hard, and we are faced with challenges that make us question ourselves and everything around us. During times like these, it takes all of our strength just to hang in there and remain whole. But somehow we survive. We persevere.

We can get into some tight places with money, for example. Our economy depends on buying and selling. We are constantly being asked to buy things, many that we can't afford or don't need. We feel bad and stressed when we bounce a check or don't have money to pay bills. Learn to become content with what you have and to live within your means. Measure prosperity differently. Perseverance is discipline.

A sister who supports her family on a limited income shared this story with pain-filled eyes. She told me about a time during the winter when her electricity was turned off. She knew she and the children would have to endure at least four days of cold and darkness. When she came home from work, her fourteen-year-old son handed her two one-hundred-dollar bills. She questioned him about where and how he got the money, and when he refused to answer she realized he was involved somehow with drugs. "I made him watch me flush the money down the toilet," she said, "and we sat down to deal with both of these stark realities." It wasn't easy, but she did the right thing. She knew somehow her family would persevere.

Perseverance is about determination. Set your goal and see yourself reaching it, knowing that you are worthy of the rewards. Visualize yourself achieving your goal. See and feel your success in your mind's eye. When we think positively, keep the faith, and believe in ourselves, we become successful. We persevere.

As you place **perseverance** on the altar, know that you are capable and worth the effort.

I am full of determination, I am worthy of reaching my goals.

"When you get in a tight place and everything goes against you till it seems as though you could not hold on a minute longer, never give up then, for that is just the time and place the tide will turn."

Harriet Beecher Stowe

Plain Talk

Parenting is one of the most important adult jobs. We have very little preparation, and it is difficult to imagine how complicated parenting can be. There are so many things to worry about! An important aspect of parenting is good communication. When you talk with your children about difficult subjects, try plain talk. It is the best way to communicate.

For example, parents worry about their children's sexual behavior. We worry because we know that they learn about sex in a haphazard manner, always being told what not to do, not being allowed to talk about it and ask questions. So many of us, when we were young, acted like sex was not important or not happening to us. Meanwhile our bodies were raging seemingly out of control with new and pleasurable feelings. Today's sexual realities are very complex, and we must accept the challenge of educating our children about them. Talking to children about sex starts early as we teach them correct names for their body parts in a no-nonsense manner. We teach them that their bodies belong to them and are sacred, private, and personal. As children mature, their questions about sex change. As parents we grow with them in answering their questions honestly. If they ask a question that shocks you or if you don't have the answer, tell them you can't answer right now, but you will get back to them. It's important that you contact someone who can help you think through an answer.

A support system for parents is invaluable. Parents learn from one another's experiences and share vulnerabilities. Sometimes our children are more comfortable discussing some issues with our close friends, who can help them become more comfortable talking to their parents. Make it as easy as possible for your child to talk to you. Set aside an hour each week to spend individually with each child for undisturbed intimate discussions.

Children grow as we guide them through life. In order to guide them effectively we must continue our own education about the realities of today's life and challenges.

As you place **plain talk** on the altar, open your mind and heart to receive the guidance given to you.

I am open to sharing with my loved ones honestly and in plain language the lessons of my life's experiences.

"Everyone and everything around you is your teacher."
Ken Keyes, Jr., *Handbook to Higher Consciousness* (1975)

Power

We all have power. Too few of us claim and use the power we have. The abuse of power makes us doubtful about using power, yet the effective use of power is a precious gift.

African American women are stereotyped as strong and powerful. Many of us don't feel that way at all. A mother of nine thought she was an inadequate wife and a bad person, who deserved to be beaten by her husband. Until she saw a television program on domestic violence in the Black community, she did not know that other Black women were abused; she thought it only happened to White women. She confided in one of her daughters who helped her seek counseling through a local shelter. Several months later she left her relationship of twenty-five years, and two years after that she and her husband sought counseling together and were reunited. She broke the conspiracy of silence, got help, connected to her power and changed her situation.

As African American women we have had to exert a lot of power just to survive and maintain our families, our livelihoods, and our health. We can recognize our power by taking a moment to look at the effect of our presence on the lives of others. Having power isn't about one person being powerful and another person being powerless. It's not about control. It's about all of us recognizing our power and realizing our capabilities. By sharing power with one another, we all grow and become powerful in our own right.

As you place **power** on your altar, feel your power all over your body.

I claim all of my personal power. I am powerful.

"It's about time for Black women to move and be moved beyond myth to power!"

Marcia Gillespie

Prayer

Prayer has saved us so much of the time. We have early memories of automatically praying that we didn't get caught for something we should not have done. Praying is something we know how to do without being taught, as if we are born knowing how to do it. As if by magic, we know what to say when we want everything to be all right or need help getting through the night. Praying is a soothing act; just talking out loud brings us hope and comfort.

The power of prayer's energy is virtually untapped in modern societies. Several years ago, a family member needed help solving a problem, so we asked friends and family around the country to light a candle and say a prayer at a specific time, to guide her in making a decision. She was able to make a clear choice and was overwhelmed by the participation and power of so many caring friends. Prayer provides a quiet, reflective time. The presence of silence helps us to think about and work on ourselves in the midst of our busy and noisy lives.

Say a silent **prayer** as you place this word on the altar.

Prayers are my connection to comfort.
I rejoice in prayer.

"I betook myself to prayer and in every lonely place I found an altar."
Elizabeth, bondswoman and minister born in Maryland, 1766

Precious
Moments

We know some moments are special while they are happening, other moments we figure it out after the fact. Precious moments lead to precious memories. These moments carry us, push us on, and make life worth living. We re-create them in our minds, because they just don't happen ever again.

Precious moments are called to my mind by some unforeseen act or presence that catches me unawares in the midst of a crowd. These unexpected retreats take me away from the present to a delicious precious moment in the past. I often think about spending a magical day with a close friend, or a terrific dancing party, or time spent with an aging relative. We have vivid memories of a special hug, glimpse, or smile from a departed loved one and we would give anything just to repeat that interaction one more time. Lucky for us we have our minds to take us to that place.

It really is a blessing that as we age we retain our long-term memory—if we didn't we wouldn't be able to recall a lifetime of precious moments, which would be a pity. Precious memories keep us going, they keep us holding our loved ones near and dear.

Put a **precious moment** on the altar flooded with love and sweet memories.

I appreciate my being full of good memories and interactions.

"Precious memories, how they linger, how they ever fill my soul."
Old Negro spiritual

Pride

We have many opportunities in life to feel proud. It's another one of those special gifts we get from the universe. When people we admire make a notable contribution or complete a phenomenal feat, our supportive participation in their activities boosts our self-esteem and makes us feel proud. We learn to feel pride as children. As youngsters, we were told that we had to represent the Negro race all of the time. We were aware that opinions were being formed about us, each and every time we were in public, and shame on us meant shame for all of our people. Racial pride was high on the agenda. Yet much of that emphasis has been lost as we have become a more integrated society. Some pride remains and is evident when we breathe a sigh of relief that a Black person was not implicated in the bombing of the World Trade Center or the Federal Building in

Oklahoma City. We care deeply about not being identified with negative behaviors. A sense of pride is a positive affirmation.

We feel a strong sense of pride when our child crosses one of life's milestones. Our children make us feel proud at school performances, with a good report card, or by a thoughtful act or deed. Graduations present many moments that allow us to experience pride and offer encouragement at the same time. I remember being surprised at the tremendous amount of pride I felt when my son got married. He accepted the commitment of marriage as a responsible adult. I was amazed that no one had told me about the immense pride the mother of the groom feels. These are feelings that warm the soul and fill us up.

Gay people have chosen to declare pride as a symbol of unhooking from the oppression of homophobia. The symbol of the rainbow, which represents the inclusion of all people regardless of ethnicity or sexuality, challenges homophobia and provides an opportunity for everyone to grow. Pride is self-respect.

As you place **pride** on the altar, reflect on a moment when you felt pride and let it fill you up.

I feel proud and I claim all of who I am.

"And he said: you pretty full of yourself ain't chu/ so she replied: show me someone not full of herself/ and I'll show you a hungry person."

Nikki Giovanni, "Poem for a Lady Whose Voice I Like" (1975)

Purple

The color purple entered my heart and my closet one day silently and unnoticed. I don't remember making the decision to wear purple everyday. It just happened. It is the color that blends with my skin, gives me energy and good luck. I love it! I wear it so much, that if I wear another color, people come up to me and ask "what's wrong?" Shopkeepers know me in the town where I live. They say here's the purple woman and I am bombarded with everything they have that's purple. I'm attracted only to purple things in stores, so much so that I had to say to myself "You don't have to buy it just because it is purple." Sometimes, after I have given a talk, sisters will come up to me and say, "I enjoyed your talk, but what color is your lipstick?" I love it. Purple is a consuming passion for some of us.

Purple puts us in touch with the part of ourselves that is regal.

Purple is the queen in all women; it helps us keep our backs straight and heads held high.

As you add **purple** to your altar, know that it touches the holy and sacred parts of you by creating power and energy.

I claim my power and I know I am a member of the royal family of the universe.

"When I am an old woman I shall wear purple."
Jenny Joseph

Reflections

Sweet Honey in the Rock sings a song about a young woman who grew up in a house where there were no mirrors. All reflections were given verbally by her grandmother, devoid of negative images and full of positive affirmations. She was not compared to anyone other than herself, and learned the art of seeing herself from an inner reflectiveness.

Parents have an opportunity and an obligation to help shape the way in which their children see themselves in the world. Attention that is focused on the positive silences the negative. Many children are given silent affirmations for proper actions and negative attention for improper actions. Many children are given reflections that mirror our frustrations and difficulties with parenting. For example, a frightened, crying child was lost in the shopping mall and brought to her mother by a security officer.

The mother immediately grabbed the child and spanked her for wandering off. This frustrated mother didn't think to hug the child or reassure her. The mother's blast of fear and anger became more important than her child's feelings. We get upset when a child breaks things, falls, ignores directions, or fights with siblings, and we forget to think about what that child might have felt or needed. It is important that the mother express her feelings in a way that lets children know she cares and is concerned about their safety.

Positive inner thoughts and feelings lead to confidence and an attitude about life that says, "I am a good and worthwhile person and I deserve the very best life offers." Inner reflections provide a stable mirror that cannot be shattered easily by external forces. We owe this foundation to ourselves and our children.

As you place **reflections** on the altar, think about the times when you have encountered an affirming mirror.

In my inner mirror I am powerful, I am good.

"You were born God's original. Try not to become someone's copy."
Marian Wright Edelman

Remembering

Most of us are able to readily recall pleasant memories. Sometimes, however, it is hard to recall unpleasant memories. We don't want to go there—it's just too much. Sometimes we have no choice and during those times we know that painful journeys are lonely, but connecting with the pain can be healing. These reflections give us the opportunity to look at our experiences with different eyes and understand their messages more clearly.

Think back to your first memories and note the feelings that emerge as you go over each detail in your mind. I have memories of being very young. One memory is from when I was four years old, standing on the porch waving good-bye to my mother as she left to teach school in Perry, Florida. Another is the birth of my brother. I can also remember the pain of getting my hair done—I have a tender scalp, and the combing and straightening of my hair was a painful ordeal. I vividly remember getting my scalp and ears burned with the curlers followed by the burning sensation from the hot Florida sun. Sometimes I can still feel the sting on my legs of being whipped with switches from the chinaberry tree. I also remember what it is like to grow up with boys who took delight in messing with my things. One day I pulled out my box with my doll in it and one of my naughty brothers had chipped the mouth away. None of them had any idea how it all happened. I was so upset. It is good to know that time and aging heal wounds.

We grew up with a saying that sticks and stones can break my bones, but words can never hurt me. That is not true: words can hurt, and hurt badly. Words can cut like swords and scar deeper than some actions. We are people whose realities are shaped and governed by words and deeds. As adults, it is important that we think again about the power of words and connect to words that have caused us pain in the past. We need to examine these sources of hurt and remove the negative power our memory has awarded them.

As you place **remembering** on the altar, pause for a moment and recall a significant past event.

I am made more powerful by being in touch with
the memories of my past.

*"What a strange thing is memory, and hope; one looks backward,
the other forward. The one is of today, the other is of tomorrow.
Memory is history recorded in our brain, memory is a painter,
it paints pictures of the past and of the day."*

Grandma Moses

Rock Bottom

These difficult words have become a part of our language as a result of the disease of addiction. Loved ones painfully wait for addicts to get to the place of making a commitment to themselves, seeking help, and entering recovery. The bottoms vary and some bottoms seem never-ending. Many of us have family members and friends who are addicted to alcohol and other substances, and whose behaviors we don't understand. We become enablers in our desire to help them recover their lives. This participation prevents them from hitting rock bottom and the addict keeps using. It is very hard to practice the tough love that is needed by addicts to reach a place where they can start recovery. Dealing with these issues and problems is a very difficult process. Help can be sought through support groups such as Naranon and Alanon.

If there is a positive side to these difficult stories, it is in the support and self-discovery of the members of support groups. I have heard many self-helpers say, "I would not have done this type of work on myself if it had not been for learning how to deal with my addict." It is as if many people find themselves by examining their relationship with the addict. They also cherish the connections and support they find in meeting and sharing with others in similar situations. These interactions speak to the isolation we feel in today's society. Most of us need people to listen to us. We need to learn from the experiences of others.

As you place **rock bottom** on the altar, say a prayer for a friend who is in the process of self-discovery and recovery.

I am worthy of having supportive love in my life. I will seek it and make it a part of my life.

"Learn to get in touch with silence within yourself and know that everything in this life has a purpose. There are no mistakes, no coincidences, all events are blessings given to us to learn."
Elisabeth Kübler-Ross

Sacred

Healing our inner selves requires that we create and claim sacred spaces. Nature provides spots that can help us cherish the simplicity and beauty of the healing process. In North Carolina I spoke at a conference that focused on creating a healing community for addicted women. The organizers chose Kanuga, an Episcopal Church camp nestled in the Blue Ridge Mountains. Kanuga Lake has a large cross on its banks which reflects in the water. A lakeside chapel makes a sanctuary for reflection and renewal. The grounds feel safe and sacred.

In our busy and stress-filled lives we must take advantage of every opportunity to commune with nature. Get away from the noise of progress and bathe in the peacefulness of calm. Take time to breathe in the fresh cleansing scents of the trees. Enjoy the gift of songs the birds offer, smell the sweetness of the flowers, and accept the blessings of beauty from the butterflies.

Sacred places can be created right in your community, whether you live in the country or the city. Visit a park and spend some time appreciating its beauty. Some churches have small gardens that can offer quiet time for reflection and rejuvenation. Create an altar and sacred place in your home. Plant a cutting garden of flowers that you love, and bring them into your bedroom to greet you when you first awaken. Flowers touch a sacred place in us.

The presence of the sacred is special because it heals our soul, feeds and nourishes our spirit. Create and claim places to pray, meditate, heal, reflect, read, write, or just be.

As you place **sacred** on the altar, realize the healing power of your altar.

I deserve a healing space. I will create and claim a sanctuary for my inner self.

"There are many, many gates to the sacred and they are as wide as we need them to be."

Sherry Ruth Anderson and Patricia Hopkins, *The Feminine Face of God* (1991)

Sexuality

Your sexuality is uniquely yours. No one else owns it, no one else defines it. It belongs to you. In order to have a healthy, wholesome life you must be in touch and accord with your sexuality. It is not okay to ignore it; it doesn't go away. It might sleep sometimes, but it does not go away. It might change what it is attracted to, or what turns it on for how long and how much, but it is always with you.

Fall in love with yourself so you can explore your sexuality, feel comfortable touching and caressing all parts of your body—yes, all parts. Learn what turns you on and enjoy how good it feels. Sexuality is a sacred part of you. It heals, releases tension, and affirms your being.

Comfort with your own sexuality allows you to be accepting of the sexuality of others. You will feel less threatened and more respectful of others' desires when you know your own sexual makeup. Sexual experiences allow you to express and give your love in tender and nourishing ways. You are always in charge of this expression. It is your most intimate gift.

As you place **sexuality** on the altar, feel the warmth of your body.

I accept my sexuality and rejoice in its nurturing and fulfilling powers.

"Sexuality is a sacrament."
Starhawk

Shalom

This Hebrew word means hello, goodbye, and peace. When we say shalom, we are saying "peace" when we arrive and "peace" when we depart. We can take peace with us wherever we go.

I went to visit a friend in North Carolina whose sister was having problems with her husband and was staying temporarily at my friend's home. The house was full of anger and frustration when I arrived. I encouraged the sister to talk about the episode leading up to her departure and, over the course of the day, she was able to verbalize her feelings. I listened to her. At the end of my two-day visit, my friend thanked me for helping to create peaceful energy in the house and helping her sister find resolve so she could return home. When we feel peace within ourselves, we are able to promote peace among others.

Peace means the same in any language: Hebrew, French, Swahili, or English. We are a diverse nation, and our challenge is to learn how to live, work, and play together. We love certain things about our diversity, such as the foods of one another's cultures. We don't think about whether or not we like Mexicans when we eat tortillas, or Jews when we eat bagels and lox. We accept their food and services, so why not the people? We must rejoice, celebrate, and respect differences. Peace brings unity and acceptance.

As we bid shalom, let's depart from each other with peace, so upon our return we will bring peace and prosperity with us.

Place **shalom** on the altar, thinking of ways that you can promote peace.

I will think of my comings and goings as
peaceful events.

"Peace is achieved one person at a time, through a series of friendships."
Fatma Reda, *The Minnesota Press* (1991)

Sister Spirit

(For Ronda)

You left us all too soon, girlfriend. We thought we had a lot of work to do together at the National Black Women's Health Project, especially when times got good. Little did we know that you were the good times: your gentle smile, your shy demeanor, your youth and willingness to do whatever needed to be done.

Somehow behind your round quiet face you kept your reality from those who loved you. Your trusting nature kept you from believing that harm could come your way. You always saw the good in everyone even when it was overshadowed with evil and destruction.

Ronda, like so many other sisters, you have left us all too soon. Too many women die every year at the hands of some jealous, crazy lunatic who still lives. Your daughter, the spitting image of you, stood at your casket for at least twenty minutes trying to make some sense of it all. Why are there no answers that can dry our tears?

We seek consolation in knowing that you were one of the sister spirits committed to the National Black Women's Health Project. We know that you have joined Ms. B. and the two of you have become powerful angels organizing all of the women who have made the transition and love the project. We know you are singing our theme song, "We are the ones." Minnie has taught it to you—she knows it very well. So when things magically start to happen, especially the events that we can't explain, we know that the three of you are working it.

We feel your energy and your gentle, sweet sister spirit walking among us. We miss you and we will keep you in our memories. Your spirit lives.

Axé and amen.

As you place **sister spirit** on the altar, think of the love you feel for a sister whose spirit lives.

I will honor the memory of a loved one through
my own actions.

"You never realize death until you realize love."
Katherine Butler Hathaway, *The Journals and Letters of the Little Locksmith*
(1946)

Sisternomics

My friend Anna works as a maid in a downtown office building. She cleans and dusts the desks of college-educated men and women, notes their comings and goings, and hears of their promotions. Anna has also sent her four children to college with little financial aid, a lot of courage, and endless faith in them and herself. Many women with more do a lot less.

Sister Akua coined the term "sisternomics" to refer to the skills of women like Anna who do big things with little money. In earlier times these women, in addition to a day's work, took in washing and ironing to make extra money. Somehow they figure out how to manage their money and take advantage of opportunities presented by the universe.

A way out of nowhere, making a lot out of a little, establishing priorities, combining discipline, wisdom, and faith. Silent prayers are constantly uttered for strength and guidance, always looking forward to a better day. This dedication promotes healing, energizes the soul, and lifts our spirit. Mothers can realize their dreams through their children's accomplishments and provide the welcomed amen, so be it, *axé*.

As you place **sisternomics** on the altar, say a prayer of thanksgiving for all of the women who made sacrifices so you could have a better day.

I am powerful and completely capable of setting a goal and reaching it.

"The fragrance always remains in the hand that gives the rose."
Heda Bejar, *Peacemaking: Day by Day*, vol. 2 (1989)

Solitude

Solitude is an adult word. You need a certain amount of security to be able to put yourself in solitude. It's easy to confuse solitude with being alone, which terrifies most of us. The fear of being alone keeps us from taking time just to be quiet. We need to have the television or stereo on, even though we are not listening most of the time. It feels as if we are afraid of ourselves or what we might learn about our being.

I am envious of people who are able to give themselves a period of solitude. Just say no to the rest of the world for a period of time, take off, and go someplace to be quiet and alone. Solitude is self-imposed; no one but you decides how the time is spent. It has to be healing just to get away from the e-mail, snail mail, faxes, telephones, voice mail, and other people's demands.

Nature gives us gifts of solitude that we can only hear when we allow ourselves to be quiet and in touch with the universe. It feels good to think about nothing sometimes.

Solitude is about cleaning out the cobwebs of your mind. It takes time and courage to go into the corners of your psyche and disentangle the confusion there. Solitude gives you time to engage in discovery and healing. Be serious, make and take time, do the work, and grow from the experience. You are a wonderful person to be alone with, so take time for solitude.

Place **solitude** on the altar knowing that it provides solace.

I am worthy of having time for solitude.

"Solitude, quality solitude, is an assertion of self-worth, because only in the stillness can we hear the truth of our own unique voices."
Pearl Cleage

Spirit

Spirit gets to the heart of things. Spirit is our inner core, our soul and our psyche. Spirit is the strength that enables us to get things done. It is an internal presence that provides us with faith and courage.

Whenever I think about the heroic feats of women such as Harriet Tubman, Sojourner Truth, Mary McLeod Bethune, and Rosa Parks, I think about the triumph of the human spirit and its ability to cross seemingly impassable boundaries. Commitment, faith, and determination ignite the spirit. We must appreciate and acknowledge this with great jubilation.

Women have a well of spirit to draw on in our families and community. The struggle of Black folks worldwide against racism and oppression speaks to the depths of our spiritual wells. We must draw from them when we feel vulnerable and challenged.

We engage in spiritual work in many ways and diverse medi-ums. Midwives and other health professionals speak of their work as a special calling, and foster parents talk about their ministry of assisting young children in need. Many of us consider our work as a ministry that feeds and nourishes the soul and spirit. Spirit and spirituality are universal concepts whose pres-ence in our lives makes the difference.

As we develop our spirituality, we are able to recognize and respect the spirituality of others. Sometimes spirit and faith are all we have, some of the time they are all we need.

As you place **spirit** on the altar, reflect on the last time you witnessed the human spirit in action.

I am a person who is in touch with my spirit and the spirit of others.

"Listening in silence helps us to experience Spirit."
Susan Taylor, *In the Spirit* (1993)

Stillness

There are times when we need to be still and reflective. Often we speak too quickly and act without forethought or thinking through a matter fully. Sometimes we need to go inward to seek solutions and guidance. When we are struggling with a problem, we contribute to the solution when we take time to be still, listen to and trust our inner voice. Many times our inner voice is our only guiding force, and we need to appreciate its presence in our lives.

The saying "Still waters run deep" often refers to a person who is quiet. I used to think that if someone was silent, they had nothing to say. I now realize that silence does not necessarily indicate a lack of thought.

We all need to become still and reflective as water, with depth and integrity that will provide us with direction. We can grow and continue to be adaptable when we are still. Inner reflection leads to positive change.

As you put **stillness** on the altar, feel the calmness in your body.

Being still and quiet brings me the calmness
my spirit needs.

"Whatever peace I know rests in the natural world, in feeling myself a part of it, even in a small way."
May Sarton, *Journal of a Solitude* (1973)

Strength

When I hear someone say that Black women are strong, the image that comes to my mind is of a large woman, carrying a large load on her head or back. This load can be anything: children, water, clothes, or other people's burdens. What I know is that this is just a stereotype, because underneath that load is a woman who is tired, a woman who is in need, and a woman who wants to be loved for who she is.

Sometimes when I am feeling especially put upon, I find it helpful to focus on the opposite of what I'm feeling. When I am having a cash flow problem, I focus on the things I am thankful for. It helps me make the decision to take steps to make sure this does not happen again. I gain inner strength from the lessons of adversity, believing that if I master this lesson I won't have to repeat it.

Tell me, what choice do we have other than being strong? Does it matter that we are tired of being strong, tired of needing to be strong? Most of us just want to sit down somewhere and be quiet, put the load down and never pick it up again.

Many of us perform daily as empty wells: we give and we give until we are empty. Create a wellspring of supportive love to help you replenish your well with nourishment and vigor. It is your responsibility to create your support systems by creating a safe place to exchange stories and energy with others. It is an affirming experience. Use your challenges as opportunity to grow.

You are strong and powerful.

As you place **strength** on the altar, connect with your inner confidence and endurance.

I recognize my own strength and am grateful for its ability to help me survive difficult times.

"Women are blessed with a jewel of strength that glows all the time."
Judith Jamison

Trees

My fondest childhood memory is of a live oak tree in our backyard. Live oaks in the South are big trees with wide, sprawling branches draped with Spanish moss. Our tree provided a perfect place for a little girl to dream. I would lie beneath the tree, gaze up at its extended arms with its long fingers, and imagine myself taking many trips to faraway places, meeting new people and doing interesting things. I hopped on the backs of leaping squirrels as they sped along branches, transporting me to private and public places. Birds' nests provided hotel space for quick stopovers or long stays. It was a multipurpose tree: it provided shelter for us to play house, a branch for a tire swing, or a protected place to wash clothes. I loved that tree. I loved dreaming in it.

A tree is a life force that provides us with a sanctuary that is often taken for granted. Trees require very little care from us, yet they give so much. We just have to take time to recognize and notice their precious gifts.

As you place the word **tree** on your altar, recall a special tree from your childhood.

I recognize the life forces of nature and their connections to me.

"The woods, tall as waves, sang in mixed / tongues that loosened the scalp."
Sonia Sanchez, *Under a Soprano Sky* (1987)

Violence

We have read, seen, and heard about violence all of our lives. It is a part of our daily living. We think about it when we go to our cars at night or in the day, when we leave and enter our homes, at school, on the playground . . . everywhere. Violence has always been with us. In order to survive, we must always be on guard.

In the late '50s, when television started to appear in our homes, Western shows were very popular. I remember hearing my mother's best friend, Mrs. Florence Henri, say, "Alyce, Matt Dillon kills someone every Saturday night." Certainly there was violence before television, but I feel that a daily dose of viewing violence makes a significant contribution to how our psyches develop.

Each of us has to examine our personal tolerance for violence.

I love movies, but I find that I have to tuck my head under my jacket during violent scenes. I am relaxed when I go to a movie and know I won't have to worry about someone being killed, raped, or maimed. Mahatma Gandhi and Martin Luther King, Jr., have taught us that the only way to end violence is through nonviolence. The prevention of violence must be taken as a personal commitment. Each of us must take some responsibility to end the violence that occurs in our families, such as spanking, yelling, sexual abuse, and psychological violence. These behaviors send the wrong messages to current and future generations.

Each of us is responsible for our own actions and for making nonviolent choices.

As you place **violence** on the altar, think of ways in which you can be less violent.

I am worthy of living in a nonviolent world. I will work to help end violence.

"Together we need to form a plan of action that will use people power. Guns don't change things; people change things."
Reverend Bernice A. King, *Hard Questions, Heart Answers* (1996)

Voice

For a long time, I tried to write about the work I've done over the past twenty-five years as a health activist. But each time I sat down to write, I would lose my voice. While I had a lot of confidence in my public-speaking abilities, I had great difficulty writing. When I tried to write in a way that I thought was acceptable, the words became flat. Powerless. Boring.

My agent, Lynn Rosen, suggested that I consider writing about another topic and suggested spirituality. Immediately I thought of *An Altar of Words*. I had built a verbal altar many times with audiences. However, when I started to write it down, I realized that I still had not silenced the voice of my ninth grade teacher telling me I would never be able to write. The written words would not come.

In the summer of '96, my partner, Ngina, and I were vacationing with some friends of the Boston Women's Health Book Collective in New Hampshire. One evening, Ngina sat me down and helped me learn to appreciate my voice. She said, "When you write, another person emerges, one who does not connect to your power and vision. Personally, I know you can write it yourself once you've made the connection." The next day Wendy, a spiritual guide, and I sat by the lake and completed a ritual where I asked the editing voice to step back and allow the spoken voice to emerge, be nourished, affirmed, and allowed to grow. That day I embarked on a journey connecting my spirit and my voice. Suddenly, everything came together, and six essays poured out of me. At dinner that evening, my friends asked me to read what I had written during the day. I shared the six essays, which are now included in this book. When I presented my work, with trembling hands, the audience responded enthusiastically, confirming that the connection had been made. After years of trying to write, finding my voice has been a liberating and affirming experience.

As you place **voice** on the altar, think about your connections to your inner thoughts and your expressions and the way you share them.

My voice is an integral part of who I am.
It connects me to all parts of my being.

*"My voice is a blessing. And no matter what other people say,
I can't block it."*

Patti LaBelle, *Don't Block the Blessings* (1996)

Water

We take water for granted. We open the tap and it flows, ready to take care of our needs. Our bodies need it to survive and we are supposed to drink eight glasses of it daily. Some of us don't like the taste of this odorless, tasteless liquid. Yet without it we perish.

As I traveled in Africa, I understood water in a different context. In the midst of the heat, what we wanted most was water, yet we were offered Fanta orange or grape sodas. Water was scarce or undrinkable. I had great trouble understanding why there was no bottled water in this area, since it could come in the same way the Fanta sodas arrived.

In most of the places we visited, women were in charge of the gardens; if a pump was not available they would bring water from nearby streams. We often saw women carrying large ewers on their heads. In areas with water pumps, crops were more plentiful and healthy. Water improved the quality of people's lives.

Being in contact with people whose lives are made difficult by the lack of water makes me appreciative of the benefits that water brings. We take so much for granted.

As you put **water** on the altar, wash your hands ceremoniously and be grateful for the life-giving and cleansing quality of water.

Water is a vital part of my life. I will appreciate it.

"You don't miss your water till the well runs dry."
Old saying

Wellness

While we hear a lot of messages and warnings about disease and prevention, we must take time to make sure that our healing is holistic. In our stressful society, it is the interconnections among our minds, our bodies, and our spirits that make us whole, well-balanced people.

Health starts first with our minds. Many of us live and survive in psychological distress, which contributes to emotional problems and if left untreated could lead to depression. Our emotional health is grossly unattended to. Our minds are meant to be healthy, not full of agony. Seek professional care if you are living with pain or unhappiness or if you are dealing with unresolved issues. Make sure your healing plan includes an evaluation of your current living and work situation, since these environments are contributing factors. You deserve peace of mind and happiness.

Physical health complements emotional health, and we need to pay special attention to diet and exercise. Stop eating fried, greasy, and rich foods. You know the healthy foods to eat—the challenge is to do it. It's hard, but you are worth the effort. If you hate to exercise, or think you don't have time, make it a priority. Figure it out. Get your yearly checkups and make them a special gift to yourself. You must fight the diseases that can destroy you and your family. You can change these conditions.

As you take more responsibility for your health, it is important to embrace wellness and spend time healing. Take a spiritual journey and make some discoveries about yourself.

Simplify your life and know that the word "no" is a complete sentence. Learn one new stress-reduction activity a month, and practice daily. Listen to music or a motivational audiotape.

Make a commitment to healing and celebrate your wellness. Feel the healing spirit as it travels through your body and forms a loving circle around you.

As you place **wellness** on your altar, create an image of your mind, body, and spirit merging, making you feel whole.

I am delighted to have wellness in my life. I will seek
it and make it an integral part of my life.
I am deserving of it.

*"Wellness also means that we take seriously our capacity to love. Learning
to fearlessly love and respect our individual and collective bodies and souls,
we can become warriors against cancer, AIDS, high blood pressure, and the
pervasive violence and stress that afflict our communities."*
Angela Davis and June Jordan, in introduction to *Body and Soul,*
edited by Linda Villarosa (1994)

Whiteness

If you ask African Americans to define whiteness, most will describe it in terms of skin color. If you ask European Americans to define blackness, most will likewise describe it in terms of skin color. We are all vulnerable here because racism has taught us life lessons about skin color. Messages are given to us in subtle and blatant ways. It starts early.

I grew up in De Land, Florida, in the 1940s. I played with a little White girl who lived on my street. Shortly after I turned six, my daddy told me that I could not play with her anymore. I was told that Colored and White children don't play together, and we could get everyone in trouble. For weeks we continued to sneak out and play together. One day we got caught and whipped for being disobedient. It didn't matter that we could not understand the senseless rules of segregation. I sometimes wonder if my ex-playmate remembers that cruel day and whether or not it made an impression on her, or made her do anything differently in her life. I, like many other Black children, suffered from the daily reminders of racism that said we were less than and not good enough for the best life has to offer. I hope that White child engaged her parents in discussions about race.

Our families had to constantly make changes to live peacefully with Whites. One year my brothers and I got skates for Christmas. Our street was unpaved and the Winn Dixie parking lot was the only place for us to skate. But our skates made too much noise and disturbed our White neighbors. There was no negotiation regarding times when we could skate. Just no skating! The White neighbors complained and I missed a developmental milestone.

We lived with fear and vulnerability in those days. White supremacy and oppression dictated every part of our lives. I remember stories of Black men being taken out into the woods and beaten by the Klan. There were many Black children who had White fathers, and there were questions about the relationships their mothers had to these men. The words rape or coercion were never mentioned. People just did what they had to do to survive.

Racism has caused us to have negative feelings about white and whiteness. We think of white skin and privilege and these thoughts immediately turn to feelings of anger, rage, and disgust. We find ourselves angry with White people, some of whom are unaware of the privileges their skin affords, since they have never been without it, and have not done any soul-searching or thinking about how race matters. It is amazing how much prominence skin color gets among supposedly intelligent human beings. In order to survive we have had to learn how to live with the dynamics of racism. We must reclaim the word "whiteness" because it has other meanings in our lives.

Blackness and whiteness are so much more than skin color. At a special screening of Julie Dash's film *Daughters of the Dust,* during a National Black Women's Health Project conference in Los Angeles, we all dressed in white. We strolled across UCLA in a grand parade, and a stunned student said, "Gosh, you all are so colorful in all of that white." Our white clothing signaled ritualistic importance; we were in a collective state of reclaiming our ancestral authenticity and power.

There are very few things that can top the cool crispness of white sheets on a hot summer night or the beauty of newly fallen snow that blankets the earth, creating a peace and serenity. On airplane rides above the clouds I love to free my mind by imagining myself sinking into the relaxing arms of white nothingness.

There are thousands of other reasons why we must reclaim this word. Remove the negative meanings that already get too much attention, and concentrate on those associations that make us feel good, and that give us comfort, peace, and power!

As you place **whiteness** on the altar, think of your favorite positive association with white and whiteness.

I claim whiteness as one of my positive words.

"No Black woman can become an intellectual without decolonizing her mind."
bell hooks

Will

When my friend Mamie was ninety-six years old, I agreed to take her from Boston to New Hampshire and Vermont to visit her granddaughter and her father's home place. Once she and I were in the car, I realized the responsibility I had assumed for such an elderly and vulnerable person. When I get upset while driving, I immediately get lost; this happens even on familiar roads. Of course, I took the wrong highway to New Hampshire and a routine two-and-a-half hour drive took nearly six hours. Mamie, however, was delighted. She loved the tour and as she recognized the towns she said, "I'm so excited, I thought I would never see this part of the world again." I relaxed and started enjoying the scenery and my incredible passenger.

Mamie was full of stories, most of them funny. She told me about the time her mother was to visit her in Concord, New

Hampshire. She got a phone call from her mother stating that she was in Concord, and Mamie was puzzled. "Are you in New Hampshire already?" "No," her mother said, "I'm in Concord, Massachusetts. Are you in New Hampshire?" Disgusted with public transportation, Mamie's mother took a taxi to Concord, New Hampshire—over ninety miles away.

In the middle of the trip I realized I was riding with history when Mamie looked casually out of the window and said, "A lot has changed in ninety-six years." I asked her what was her secret to a long life, and she said she loved her independence and she took her medicine every night. As we approached the New Hampshire border we saw a state liquor store, and she said, "This is where I get my medicine." I saw her independence and will as I helped her get out of the car so she could make her own purchases. In the liquor store people looked at her with admiration and amazement.

We arrived at her granddaughter's home in the midst of the first snowfall of the year. Mamie was amused at my delight with the snow and told me she had seen hundreds of snowfalls. We visited her father's home place in Windsor, Vermont, as she told us stories about her visits over ninety years ago.

I learned so much about willpower that weekend, from watching her climb three floors, resting on each floor, so she could see her granddaughter's bedroom. Her will to live her life as she wanted to (with respect) was evident. She endured mistreatment by caretakers who talked about her as if she were not there, and yet her strong will to live provided a lesson for us all.

As you place **will** on the altar, be in touch with your innermost desires and allow your willpower to encircle those desires.

I am powerful and feel connection to my inner will.

"Where there is a will, there is a way."
Old saying

Wisdom

Much of our wisdom comes at our kitchen tables. We listen to grownups telling the stories of their lives and we gain wisdom from them. When I was a child, I always knew the good part of a story was about to be shared when they told me to go outside and play. I wanted to hear, so I would start playing the game of coming back inside requesting everything from a glass of water to a Band-Aid. I wanted to listen to their stories.

As an adult I treasure the times when I can gather in the kitchen with friends or family and share our stories. There is much wisdom in talking about issues that are of concern to us. Each kitchen table session over the years has included the sharing of the wisdom of life lessons learned by women. We come away with our souls nourished and full of wisdom.

Children are capable of sharing wisdom through the clarity of their innocence. The day before my husband's death, we were traveling from my mother's house in Jacksonville to Gainesville, Florida, where we lived. As we left, my mother said to Wesley, "Be careful on the highway and call me when you get home." My husband said, "Who me? I plan to live until I'm a hundred!" Our son, Wesley, age seven, looked up at his dad and said, "How can you be so sure?" The question stuck in my mind and that was the only sign I had that my husband would die of a heart attack the next day.

Wisdom comes from many places and many people. It is a gift of the ordinary. Many of the "old wives' tales" and practices contain bits of truth within them. If we listen we can hear voices of wisdom whispering in our ears.

There is much wisdom available; use it and grow.

As you place **wisdom** on the altar, make a pledge to listen for its truthful voice.

I delight in being full of wisdom and will share
my bounty with others.

*"We have rarely been encouraged and equipped to appreciate the fact that the
truth works, that it releases the Spirit and that it is a joyous thing."*

Toni Cade Bambera